The Ultimate Guide to Starting a Freelance Web Design Business

Contents

Acknowledgments

Thanks to Cory Miller, Kevin D. Hendricks, Kristen Wright and James Dalman for the writing, editing and publishing help. Thanks to Jared Atchison, Brian Casel, Dave Clements, Carrie Dils, Bill Erickson, Dan King, Curtis McHale, Andrew Norcross and Justin Sainton for sharing their freelance insights. Last, but not least, a big thanks to Cody Smith for the cover and print layout design.

Introduction

I remember the nervousness and anxiety when I landed my first freelance web design client way back in 2007.

It was quite daunting to take someone's money for work that I was still learning to do (even if I was charging $25 an hour for the project).

I knew little to nothing about the ins and outs of freelancing, like accounting, project management and client work. So I had to learn fast.

I didn't realize that working from my dining room table and my wicker chairs would cause me back problems. Or that working a full-time job, then coming home and continuing to my freelance work into the early hours of the night would leave room for little else in my life and if I kept going at that pace, a big crash and burn.

But that initial journey was all worth it though because I was chasing a dream.

Freelance web design meant something bigger to me: Freedom.

My dream initially wasn't to change the world, but to change just mine.

(In addition to paying off debt, I was living in an apartment and wanted to buy a house so all the money I made went to a downpayment — oh, and taxes).

But my dreams soon became bigger as I got more and more work and increased my rates. My dreams grew to include a new career and ultimately the opportunity to be a full-time entrepreneur. (And yes, to make a difference in my little corner of the world, one client at a time.)

Freelancing was the key to all of this. It enabled me to pursue and achieve these dreams and more.

I'm so glad I took that first client project and got past my fears and anxieties. I'm so grateful I made the sacrifices I did back then because it's gotten me to where I am now ... and the freedom I enjoy today.

Because of my freelancing work, I was able to start iThemes in 2008 and since then serve other freelance web designers, building high-quality WordPress products, tailored for them and their clients.

So even though I'm no longer a freelancer, I have a special place in my heart for those on the journey of freelance web design.

This is why we've published this book: to help you and others starting the journey of building a freelance web design business.

We've taken the key areas I and other rookie freelancers have struggled with and given you tips and guidance for learning how to be happy, healthy and successful as a freelance web designer.

Additionally, throughout the book we've shared stories of successful freelancers to inspire you. (Yes, you can do it too!)

I wish this book existed in 2007. I would have felt less nervous and been less anxious.

I would have been better prepared for the ups and downs. It would have been my desktop reference as I waded through what it really meant to be a solid freelance web designer.

I hope this book is a handy companion and guide as you get your freelance web design business going.

And as you take your first steps, I wish you the best ...

—Cory Miller
Founder
iThemes.com

P.S. — Along the way, if you find this book helpful, or have a question or two, I'd love it if you sent me an email telling me how it's going. You can send those to cory@ithemes.com.

Ready to Go Freelancing?

The world is shifting. Once upon a time our parents or grandparents landed a job and expected to stay there. Forever. Those days are gone. Not only do people switch jobs like a game of hot potato, but more and more people have gone freelance.

A new study[1] shows that 53 million Americans are now doing freelance work. OK, that's a big number. So what?

That's 34% of the workforce.

1 in 3 working people are freelancers.

This is a big shift in the economy. Some see it as a good thing:

"A more nimble economy is potentially more innovative, more competitive, and better able to deal with the fluctuations of global markets." (Freelancing in America[2])

---

1   https://www.freelancersunion.org/blog/
dispatches/2014/09/04/53million/

2   www.forbes.com/sites/laurashin/2014/09/08/1-in-3-american-workers-
freelances-but-is-the-phenomenon-growing/

Some see it as something to worry about:

Independent workers "don't have the workforce protections that have developed over the last 80 years. They are simply on their own," said Robert Reich, the Secretary of Labor under President Bill Clinton and now a professor at the University of California, Berkeley. (Wall Street Journal[3])

And some see it as more than a big change. They're describing it as the greatest thing since sliced bread:

"But this is more than an economic change. **It's a cultural and social shift on par with the Industrial Revolution.** Just as the move from an agrarian to an industrial society had dramatic effects on social structures around civil rights, workforce participation, and even democracy itself, so too will this shift to a more independent workforce have major impacts on how Americans conceive of and organize their lives, their communities, and their economic power." (emphasis mine, Freelancing in America[4])

Yes, going freelance is a big deal.

Who's Freelancing?

It used to be that tracking how many people were freelancing was a simple matter—they're either freelancing or they're not. But these days it's a lot more complicated. Only 40% of freelancers are what we traditionally think of as freelancers. There's a huge group—27%—that still has a regular job and is just moonlighting.

---

3   blogs.wsj.com/atwork/2014/09/04/one-in-three-u-s-workers-is-a-freelancer/

4   https://www.freelancersunion.org/blog/dispatches/2014/09/04/53million/

Then there are folks cobbling together an income from multiple jobs, the temporary workers and the small business owners who function like freelancers.

Here's the breakdown:

WHO ARE ALL THESE FREELANCERS?

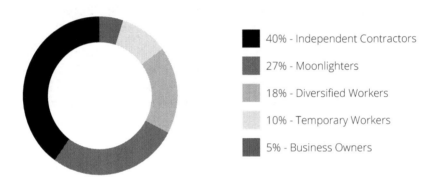

- 40% - Independent Contractors
- 27% - Moonlighters
- 18% - Diversified Workers
- 10% - Temporary Workers
- 5% - Business Owners

The workforce in general—and freelancing specifically—has changed a lot since our parents' day. The idea of diversified workers—stitching together an income (and probably health insurance) from several sources—is new.

It's not quite the traditional job market of the past.

So Why Go Freelance?
If this is all new and different, why do it? Here are the top reasons freelancers give[5].

5   www.forbes.com/sites/laurashin/2014/09/08/1-in-3-american-workers-freelances-but-is-the-phenomenon-growing/

Top 10 Personal Motivations for Freelancing:
1. 68% – To earn extra money.
2. 42% – To have flexibility in my schedule.
3. 37% – Out of financial necessity.
4. 33% – Ability to choose my own projects.
5. 31% – To be in control of my own financial future.
6. 30% – To be able to pursue work I am passionate about.
7. 30% – To gain additional skills or experience.
8. 29% – To be able to spend more time with friends and family.
9. 27% – To have independence from things such as office dynamics.
10. 22% – To expand my professional network.

Sounds like **money**, **flexibility** and **control** are the big reasons.

And it's paying off with happy freelancers.

Freelancers Are Happier
While a changing economy and technology and all that other stuff get the attention in this shifting transition to freelance, what really matters is how people feel about their work.

We spend nearly half our waking lives at work. You might as well enjoy it. And freelancers do (according to the Field Nation infographic[6]):

90% of freelancers are satisfied or very satisfied with their work.
Verses the 65% of full-time workers who are unsatisfied or somewhat unsatisfied with their jobs.

Ouch.

---

6   www.fieldnation.com/wp-content/uploads/2014/09/1408_infographic-field-nation-american-workforce-contractors_v3D.jpg

But the numbers don't end there.

Full-time workers aren't just dissatisfied, they're not doing great work. All that negativity is bringing things down:

70% of employees are disengaged from their work. It's estimated those disengaged employees cost the U.S. $450 to $550 billion a year. These crabby employees are a bad influence, they skip work, drive away customers and steal on the job (*Office Space* anyone?).

Meanwhile the freelancers are happy: **96% of freelancers are committed to the company they work for.**

There's more:

60% of employees feel they should have chosen a different career. **But 88% of freelancers wouldn't switch to a typical 9-to-5 job.**

Noticing the trends? **Freelancers tend to be happier, more productive and more dedicated.** They find purpose and meaning in their work, and in the end everybody wins.

Ready for Freelancing Success?

Now let's be realistic. Not every traditional, full-time employee hates their job and steals paper clips. **Some people do love their jobs.** Not everyone is jumping the sinking ship of full-time corporate employment. But it is becoming more common. One-third of the American workforce is a big deal.

Oh, and that crowd of freelancers will just get bigger[7]: By 2020, freelancers are expected to make up 50% of the full-time workforce.

---

7   www.forbes.com/sites/groupthink/2013/11/25/how-an-exploding-freelance-economy-will-drive-change-in-2014/

And there is that mountain of research showing that freelancers are **happier**.

So if you're not loving your job, if you're not happy with what you're doing and where you're at, maybe it's time to start thinking about going freelance.

Why WordPress?

So freelancing is looking more and more attractive. Now let's talk WordPress. **Why should you make WordPress the center of your web design business?**

WordPress started in 2003. It's been around for more than a decade.

WordPress is now powering more than 20% of the web[8].

WordPress is powering 52 of the top 100 blogs.

But it's not just for blogging—69% use WordPress as a content management system.

All of that means WordPress is a sold platform for building websites. It's stable. It's secure. It's mature. It's not going to disappear when some net giant gobbles it up. It's not some weird system nobody knows—it's practically mainstream.

WordPress is flexible with themes and plugins. You can do a simple basic website or power a giant ecommerce store. It can do pretty much anything your clients need.

There are a lot of hosted services these days promising fancy features. But they take control away from people.

---

8   http://w3techs.com/technologies/overview/content_management/all

With WordPress you can give your clients ownership.

Unlike other complicated content management systems, WordPress is designed to be easy to use. Posting content is as simple as writing an email or working on a Word doc.

You probably know all this, but it's important to reiterate. WordPress is a solid platform, and you need to be prepared to make that case to your clients.

Story: Why WordPress

CARRIE DILS, FREELANCE DEVELOPER

What prompted you to become a freelancer and specifically work with WordPress?

I've done a ton of freelance work in the past and have always enjoyed the autonomy of working from home as well as the flexibility to work projects of my choosing. Once I was introduced to WordPress and realized how much more quickly I could knock out websites for clients, I was sold.

Also, as a one-person shop, I can't possibly know or do it all, so it's appealing to work with software that's under such active development. WordPress gives me the best of both worlds in terms of starting off with a solid code base but being able to build on that with my code.

Philosophy

The first step to freelancing is to get your head in the right space. There's a certain philosophy to freelancing. It's a mindset. **It's a way of thinking that's decidedly different than working for *the man* in a cubicle.**

We'll get to business plans, budgets and branding. But first we need to talk about this philosophy of freelancing and why you want to be a freelancer.

We'll start with a lot of that big picture thinking—being happy at work, finding purpose, seeking change, having the right motivation. Then we will get practical as we talk about money, relationships that can help and options for the freelance transition. Then we'll take some time for self evaluation—asking yourself a lot of questions.

Going freelance is a seismic shift. It's big. Before you take that leap, let's make sure you know what you're getting into and that it's a good fit.

Happy at Work, Happy in Life

In the book *Wellbeing: The Five Essential Elements*, which is based on Gallup research, author Tom Rath and Jim Harter write:

"People usually underestimate the influence of their career on their overall wellbeing. But Career Wellbeing is arguably the most essential of the five elements. If you don't have the opportunity to regularly do something you enjoy—even if it's more of a passion or interest than something you get paid to do—the odds of your having high wellbeing in other areas diminish rapidly.

People with high Career Wellbeing are more than twice as likely to be thriving in their lives overall." (emphasis mine)

Career happiness overflows into every other area of your wellbeing and life.

Think about it: **How may chronically unhappy, miserable people do you know who just absolutely love their job?**

Anybody come to mind? Probably not.

Be happy at work, be happy in life.

We spend more time at work than at home. More time with coworkers and bosses than with our family and friends.

So why aren't we more deliberate, methodical, strategic and focused on finding meaningful work?

Work that pays the bills but also frees us to be fulfilled and happy in our jobs. We should pursue work that not only meets our physical needs, but also meets our emotional and spiritual needs as well. You're going to spend a vast chunk of your life at work, it might as well be work that matters.

That's what we call a **purposeful paycheck**. It's something you can find in any job you love, but it most often happens with entrepreneurs and freelancers who strike out on their own to pursue what they love.

One of the major reasons to strike out as a freelancer is to find purpose and happiness in your work. Being your own boss, setting your own agenda and pursing the work you love (and getting paid for it) is a big draw to the freelance life.

More than just another way to pay the bills, there's a mindset to freelancing. It's a freelancing philosophy.

Understanding and embracing this way of thinking can bring a new motivation to your freelance journey.

Hardest, Greatest Thing Ever

Starting your own freelance career is a bold step in entrepreneurship. Let's be clear about that. You're not just doing some projects on the side. You're starting your own business. **You are an entrepreneur.**

And you need to understand something about entrepreneurship: it's a journey. A long, hard, challenging one. And not for the faint of heart.

Entrepreneurship is like scaling the summits of legendary peaks like Mount Everest or Kilimanjaro.

Like those climbing expeditions, there are great risks and rewards in entrepreneurship. There are trials and tribulations along the path to the summit. It's filled with deep valleys and tall peaks. The terrain is mostly rocky and requires constant focus, energy and direction.

Instead of death, the risks of entrepreneurship are more related to financial damage or ruin and tend to affect the freelancer as well as their families and those of the people involved directly in the businesses.

Yet the rewards are similar. There is the challenge of the task, one few approach and even fewer can handle.

It's the pursuit of a passionate adventure, using your time, talent and treasure to make your mark on the world.

Freelance expeditions are also filled with heroic and/or horrific results.

Entrepreneurship requires great preparation and a sound initial plan, focused purpose and passion, and typically involves a team of people to make it all happen.

Budding freelancers need to understand:

Entrepreneurship is the hardest job you'll ever have. Wusses need not apply.

At the same time:

It's also the most fulfilling, fun, challenging and rewarding job you'll ever have.

Entrepreneurs, like the world's bravest mountain climbers, are a different breed from normal civilians. Most entrepreneurs aren't suited for typical work. In fact, after they start their first businesses, they are often ruined for normal employment or realize they were never meant to pursue the journey of entrepreneurship in the first place.

Successful freelancers have a compelling vision and dream that stirs them and keeps them up at night. They have forward motion, an unmatched drive and initiative for life in the pursuit of their bold goals.

They see a way to make the world a better place, or at least their small corner of it.

As Steve Jobs said, we entrepreneurs want to "make a dent in the universe."

Before you embark on the journey, you need to make sure it fits who you are and where you want to go in life.

Lao-Tzu said: "The journey of a thousand miles begins with a single step."

Are you ready for that first step?

Story: High School Dropout

JUSTIN SAINTON, FREELANCE DEVELOPER, ZAO

The high school dropout story is often a cautionary tale, but for freelance WordPress developer Justin Sainton it's worked out just fine. He quit high school early and got his GED so he could launch his own web development company, Zao. That was 2004 and he's still going strong today.

His first web experience came in 1998 when he was 12: "I used Adobe GoLive and made $100 building a website for a skateboarding company," he said. "At 12 years old that feels like you're the richest guy in the world, so that planted the seed in me that I could do this web thing." That early web entrepreneurship sounds like the stories we championed in our free Kids Creating Stuff Online ebook.

Justin completely bypassed college and hasn't looked back. He got into WordPress in 2007 and today specializes in ecommerce.

Finding Purpose in Our Paychecks

"If a man is called to be a street sweeper, he should sweep streets even as Michelangelo painted, or Beethoven composed music, or Shakespeare wrote poetry. He should sweep streets so well that all the hosts of heaven and earth will pause to say, here lived a great street sweeper who did his job well." -Martin Luther King Jr.

If you're going to do anything, do it in a way that all others will watch and admire because of your passion, dedication and energy.

As a freelancer, people will take notice of how you approach everything do. Yes, everything from how you treat the receptionist when meeting a client to delivering excellent websites with every detail nailed perfectly.

That kind of commitment requires tremendous purpose in the work you do.

If you want to be a successful freelancer, you have to realize that these aren't just jobs. **You can't just earn a paycheck with a shrug of the shoulders.**

We should approach our work in a way that, regardless of whether you have a brush and canvas or a broom and dustpan, people would say your work *is* art.

Find deeper purpose in your work. Discover that internal motivation that will shine through in your work, help you stand out from the crowd and keep you in business. Because as a freelancer, it's all on you (no pressure).

Changing When It Sucks

If you're not loving your current job, it's time to change. Hopefully that's why you're considering freelancing. Well, it's OK to quit your job. (Do it responsibly of course, but more on that later.)

We're not slaves to a lifestyle or a job or a boss. We have the privilege of changing it when it sucks.

Happiness in your work is *your* responsibility.

No one says you have to stay if you're unhappy. Those most bitter or unhappy at work are often trapped. The result? The Bitter Bobs and Bettys of the world.

So if we can't find happiness, satisfaction or even contentment in what we're doing then we need to change before we get bitter.

Change itself sucks. No one ultimately likes change. But bitterness is worse.

Bitterness will suck the life out of you and kill you from the inside out. It will poison your relationships, your outlook on life and rob you of your physical health.

Change is a funny thing. It is the thing we hate to do, and we often let the status quo go far too long before making actual steps to make a change. Oftentimes, change happens, when others do it for us. But it is absolutely, unequivocally vital for our career happiness.

We have to be willing to change when the time comes.

Now be warned you will be unhappy for seasons even in the best roles and environments. It's part of life. We don't always get to do what we want.

But happiness is your responsibility. Commit to making the changes when necessary to put yourself on the right track again. Or find yourself lost, trapped and drowning in a sea of bitterness and misery.

Choose change over bitterness.

Freelancing might not be the answer to everything, but if your job situation sucks then it's time to change.

Story: Change

CORY MILLER, FOUNDER, ITHEMES

Bitterness can suck the life out of you. I've seen it happen.

One of my first jobs out of college, I worked with a person who had been at that organization my entire life. Since before I was born in fact. And when I arrived she had long ago stopped learning and growing. She had stagnated and was stuck. She had neglected to keep up with technology and was hanging on to what little she had left that allowed her to make a meaningful contribution to the team and organization. She made just a little above minimum wage at the time. And she was bitter and miserable.

By extension, she made everyone else miserable. No one wanted to be around her. As I worked with her for over a year, witnessing how the bitterness had eaten away at her youth and poisoned the air around her, I vowed never to get to that point.

It made a lasting impact on me and I've never forgotten it. So whenever I've been in positions where I felt a dead end coming or could not stomach the energy to work with the people who were my bosses, I chose to change my situation rather than go down the road to bitterness and poison.

I wanted to do more with my life and the few resources and little time I have. I promised myself to be ready to change if I ever felt the prison of a job or situation trapping me.

Thirst for Learning

Most unhappy people stopped learning long ago. They think they magically arrived one day because they accomplished some marker in life (like a college degree, raise or promotion).

But freelancers love learning. Life is absolute and unending curiosity for us. **We yearn to learn.**

You should always be seeking to learn and grow, and add new skills and experiences to your resume so you are more valuable for yourself and for your teams, customers and clients.

Learning and growing gives us the edge by keeping us *on* the cutting edge. **To stop learning is to whither and die.** And we seek to live fruitful and fulfilled lives that come through the nonstop journey of learning.

Lifelong learning is about investing in yourself. It's an investment you take with you regardless of the position or organization you're with. So it's not wasted—it only makes you more of a star free agent in your field!

One of the keys to learning and investing in yourself is doing it on your own time and dime.

This means you:

• **Don't rely on your employer to invest in you.** You can't count on others to care about your growth—and you shouldn't!

• **Invest in yourself on nights and weekends.** You shouldn't think you can do all this primarily at your day job. The key to earning more and being more valuable is a personal investment which means investing your time "off the clock." The rising stars in our organization are the ones committed to learning, who make the sacrifice and investment on their own time.

- **Do the hard work to continue to sharpen your skills and learn more.** It is hard work to keep sharpening your sword and adding more arrows to your quiver. This is often a big stumbling block to self-directed learning—it takes effort. Take the first step and you'll set yourself apart.

- **Open your own wallet.** Yes, this means you might need to pay for a nighttime course at the local university or to sit for a certification exam or purchase an online course or training membership. But again, it's an investment in yourself that you take with you. And aren't you worth the investment? As a career free agent, aren't you worth that time and money?

- **Be intentional, proactive and strategic about learning.** It won't come easy, it won't come cheap and it will cost you time. But in the end you'll be more valuable and sought after as a result.

Do you want to know the easiest, most affordable way to learn?

It's called reading.

Start a reading addiction today. Don't just start a reading habit. A habit is something you do normally, even subconsciously, so much that you don't even realize it's a habit. Start an addiction where you're craving new information and growth that can only be satisfied by buying books and devouring them on a regular basis.

Great books are the collected wisdom of experts who have taken the time and energy to articulate their ideas, experiences and expertise in a digestible format. Instant knowledge! They've gone through several editors and others who help make them even better. **You get all the benefit for a fraction of the cost.**

Books are goldmines for your learning. Just because you think you can't read or have a different learning style doesn't mean you shouldn't *try* to read — and read regularly. (And of course there are usually audio versions of most books for your daily commute!)

With today's technology you have access to a world of books in the palm of your hand, wherever you go. Learning doesn't have to be something formal where you sit at a desk. It can happen anywhere. With that kind of an attitude you can always be learning, always growing, always getting one step ahead.

Don't Do It for the Wrong Reasons

The freelance journey is like a roller coaster. It can be filled with the highest of highs and the lowest of lows. You might want to throw up afterward (or worse, during). At some point you might beg to get off this crazy ride. At other points you might throw your hands up and squeal like a little girl (that's a good thing).

We're going to be honest here because you need to know what you're getting into. This is your life and we can't sugarcoat it. **Some call freelancing an adventure. For others, it's a nightmare.**

The Right Motivation for the Journey

If you don't set out on the freelance journey with the motivation and a clear understanding of the goal, your journey could be a disaster, with potential financial ruin for you and your family.

In other words, if you're stepping on to the roller coaster ride for the wrong reasons, prepare to see your dinner come up!

With that, here are several misconceptions or poorly directed motivations for going freelance:

Getting Rich

Going freelance is a great way to build wealth. It breaks through the glass ceiling of a limited hourly rate or salary. If you work harder, you can make more.

However, **if money is your sole motivation, you're likely going to be miserable.** (And the business failure statistics prove the odds aren't in your favor.)

The odds of getting wildly rich are stacked against you. Once your business starts generating cash to pay bills and salaries, you'll quickly learn the term "cash flow." This means you need cash to pay those bills and salaries, which means you'll have to keep a certain amount of money in the business bank account and won't be able to take it out. Just like retail outlets need a certain amount of cash in the register to make change, you've also got to have cash to run your business. Otherwise, no cash means no air for your business. And you're done.

It's OK to want to earn more money. But if that's your primary motivation, then you might be in trouble.

Being Successful Overnight

For those who think success is built overnight, you're chasing a myth. No one sees all the hard work, contacts and relationships, ingredients and skills, dumb luck and circumstances that went into the "overnight" successes we hear about today. That sexy sound bite is inspiring. It sounds amazing. But it glosses over the years of failure, the 80-hour-work weeks and the vast majority who tried the same thing and never made it.

If you expect this to be a quick journey, you'll get a little winded and raise your heart rate a bit, think again. This is a marathon. Most people quit. A lot of the finishers puked their guts out at mile 13.

Ultimate and Complete Freedom and Flexibility

Many freelancers toil under other people for years, yearning for the day when they can get their freedom and chart their own course. They want unhindered autonomy, complete flexibility of schedule and being free of the cubicle or chains of typical employment. It's a compelling vision.

But the reality is in the first years at least you'll be attempting to get your dream off the ground. You might be working six or seven days a week and a minimum of 60 hours per week. You might get to set that schedule, but choosing your start time is small comfort when you work 12 hours in one day.

As the chief firefighter in charge, you now get the phone calls at 2 a.m. Or when you're on the road courting new business something bursts into flame and you have to deal with it.

You'll likely have more freedom and flexibility than before. But it won't be complete, unhindered or without accountability. You still have clients, your family, maybe partners and perhaps employees you are responsible to and for.

Being Your Own Boss

Or not having a boss ever again. But the reality is as a freelancer you trade one boss for many more. They are just called clients now. As a freelancer, you greatly multiply your new bosses. If you don't understand your clients or serve them, they will vote you out of business by taking their money elsewhere. If you don't please them, they will fire you. And it's much easier for them to fire you than it was your old boss. Think about it—they don't have to pay unemployment insurance, worry about workplace discrimination or even be kind to you as they fire you. They can often do it without reason and without warning (contracts can sometimes help).

Of course you have the freedom to fire them too. And you should fire bad clients. But you always have to weigh the risk. Your clients pay your bills, so it's something you need to think through carefully.

Story: Wrong Reasons
CORY MILLER, FOUNDER, ITHEMES

Our company, iThemes, was named the seventh fastest growing company in Oklahoma City after three years in business. It was an awesome honor (especially when compared to high-growth industries like our oil and gas exploration industry), but I know our success didn't happen magically in three short years (*or* simply on my own talent!).

Personally, I spent over 15 years building my personal skills—reading dead trees, listening, watching, growing and learning from anyone I could. I collected a ton of experience under bad leadership to learn what I didn't want to do, and ultimately found partners who shared my same values. All of that played into our success. I also recruited or stumbled onto an amazing team that helped us get there! (And, by the way, we're still not there!)

Overnight successes don't exist.

Money Mindset
Let's talk about the philosophy of freelance finances. Maybe you'll make more money as a freelancer (and maybe not). But before thinking about riches, you need to get the right mindset about money.

What you want is **financial freedom**.

Freedom to do what you want without the financial baggage of debt that forces you to stay in a job you simply hate.

Too often we chase material wealth instead of meaningful work and the result is emptiness, lost opportunities and regret.

When you take a job *just* because of the financial lifestyle upgrade you can get with it or to support your lavish material cravings, you're choosing an almost certain path to misery. The money is so good it covers up the fact that you really hate the work.

Money can become a prison cell, shackling you to a miserable job with "golden handcuffs".

People find themselves in these situations and they can't get out of it. They've got a mortgage and a car payment and credit card debt— all financial obligations weighing them down. They don't have the freedom to take a lower paying job, even if it's something they'd love.

We inadvertently trade purpose and meaning and impact for wealth and material possessions. Sadly we're trading in a real lasting legacy for things that rot and decay. You never see a U-Haul behind a hearse.

If you can say no to the greed and just meet your need, you'll discover tremendous financial freedom. You won't be chained by debt and you'll be able to take risks and pursue work you love.

Yes, you need to meet your financial obligations. You need to eat, pay rent or whatever. But when we stack things on top of those basic needs and raise that bar above reality it can suffocate us.

What is your true need? What goes over the line into outright greed? It's something you'll have to answer for yourself.

Here are few tips for financial freedom that can get you started:

- **Fix your mindset about money and material wealth.** Manage money—don't let money manage you.

- **Stop spending more than you earn.** It's pretty simple. If you're spending more than you earn or getting over your head into debt you're starting to build your own prison cell.

- **Start a budget.** Know where your money goes. This is the key. Set it down and get it on paper (or pixel). Whether you use Mint.com or something else, you need to know where your money goes.

- **Get accountability for the gaps and weak areas.** You'll have blind spots and areas where you need help. You and your significant other need to be *synced* on this issue. Also that person is often the best one to help keep you on the straight and narrow!

- **Get on the debt snowball.** Start paying off your debts, one by one, starting with the smallest one and rolling those extra payments onto the bigger ones.

- **Stay there. Enjoy the freedom.** Once you've achieved financial freedom, the key will be maintaining that freedom. It's too easy once you're free to jump back into overspending, so make a plan to get financially free and stay financially free.

Are you serious about your financial freedom? Then get Dave Ramsey's book *Total Money Makeover*. Start reading it and implementing his baby steps to financial freedom. Then find a Financial Peace University group in your area and join it. You'll appreciate knowing you aren't alone, and the accountability and cheerleading will be a big boost.

We'll talk more about finances later, but this is a first step. This is a foundational philosophy you need to embrace as a freelancer. **Very few freelancers make it when they're burdened with too much debt.**

Relationships

Freelancing can be a lonely business. You're often working at home, by yourself, getting little interaction with the outside world. Freelance relationships are hard to come by. Which is a problem, because **relationships drive freelancing**.

You need all kinds of connections to make your living—you need clients to hire you, collaborators to work with and specialists to do what you don't do. **You need freelance relationships to succeed.**

What about companionship and self-improvement? Even the introverts need to connect with other people from time to time. And you need to interact with others to get better—iron sharpens iron. **You need freelance relationships to survive.**

Why Freelance Relationships Matter

Why are people so important to your freelance business? Three reasons:

1. Getting work.
2. Getting help.
3. Getting better.

Getting Work

You get freelance work through relationships. That's simply how it works.

According to the Freelancers Union[9], the top source of work for freelancers is word of mouth (53%) followed closely by personal contacts (51%). People talk. You get work. It's as simple as that.

---

9   https://www.freelancersunion.org/blog/
dispatches/2014/09/04/53million/

So you need to cultivate those relationships. Your happy clients talk to potential clients. They recommend you. Word spreads. Or someone needs a job done and rather than Google it, they ask their friends. They'd rather find a professional through their trusted network.

This is the web of freelance relationships and it's how you're going to make money.

And it's not just clients who talk. Freelancers do too. Another study from the Freelancers Union[10] found that 81% of freelancers refer work to other freelancers.

When it comes to finding work, it's all about freelance relationships.

Getting Help

One thing you're going to learn pretty quickly as a freelancer is that you can't do it all. You don't know everything and you don't have time for everything. At some point you're going to need help.

This happens in several ways:

- **Pro Services** – You're a web developer. You're not a writer or an accountant or a plumber. The hours you would spend doing your taxes might be better spent doing the web work you're good at. Yes, it might be cheaper dollar-wise to do your own plumbing, but the stress and time might make hiring a plumber a brilliant investment.

- **Sub-Contracting** – If you're a successful freelancer, you're going to get busy. There may come a time when you're way too busy.

---

10   https://www.freelancersunion.org/blog/dispatches/2014/07/01/
freelance-life-survey-report/

You need to bring in some help to get the job done. You hire a few other freelancers to tackle parts of the job (the parts you like least).

- **Referrals** – Freelancing is becoming a pretty niche business, as it should be. Specialized freelancers are highly successful. There are very few generalists these days. The end result is you're going to have clients who aren't a good fit. Their project might be too big or too small for you. Maybe they want a platform you don't know very well.

- **A good freelancer will recognize when a client isn't a good fit and refer them to someone else.** This is why 81% of freelancers refer work to other freelancers. Not only are you helping out your freelance friend, you're providing good service to a potential client. They're not a good fit as a client today, but who knows when that will change or who else they'll talk to. But you've made a good impression.

Hiring professional services, sub-contracting work and giving referrals all require relationships. You need to know other freelancers to recommend when a client isn't a good fit. You need to know an accountant to hire. You need to know other coders you can hire to sub-contract. So you better build up those freelance relationships.

Getting Better

Finally, freelance relationships matter because you need them to get better. It's by interacting and connecting with others that we're challenged and forced to improve.

Our suppositions are questioned and we have to defend ourselves or reconsider our position.

Friends can help us improve our skills and point to new ideas we hadn't considered. How many times has a friend turned you on to the latest and greatest new thing?

Sometimes you need that gentle push from someone you trust to make your work that much better.

Iron sharpens iron.

Your livelihood and sanity depend on freelance relationships. As you consider stepping out into the freelance world, find some friends for the journey.

Story: Do What You're Good At

KEVIN D. HENDRICKS, FREELANCE WRITER, MONKEY OUTTA
NOWHERE

The best freelance advice I've ever received is to hire experts to do whatever I'm not good at. When I launched my freelance business that included hiring a lawyer to set up my legal entity and turning to an accountant come tax time. My tax guy especially has been a sanity saver.

I hate math. Crunching numbers is just not something I enjoy doing. Pair that with sorting through the bureaucracy of the IRS and you've got my own personal nightmare.

Prior to launching my own business I had done my taxes a few times. Even with the help of tax software I still spent at least six hours struggling with paperwork. When I managed to finish I was never confident I'd done it right, and I was not someone my wife wanted to be around.

So when I started my freelance business and added all those extra tax complications, hiring an expert was a no-brainer.

In the end I save time and money—the hours I would spend doing it myself are better spent working at my hourly rate doing what I'm good at. That more than pays for hiring my accountant. Plus I save myself the frustration and have the confidence to know my taxes were done right and the IRS won't come calling.

Get help in your freelance business from professionals who know what they're doing—whether it's accountants, lawyers or even plumbers. (I make more money writing than I could ever save by trying to fix a problem myself and refusing to call an expert.) You'll be glad you did.

The Transistion

Leaping into freelance work is pretty popular these days. One-third of the U.S. workforce is freelancing[11] in some form or another. But look before you leap, and plan your freelance transition. Jumping without a parachute is not recommended (though some people thrive on risk).

The freelance transition can be pretty rough. Those direct deposit paychecks no longer magically appear every two weeks, keeping your bank account fat and happy. Instead, income is inconsistent and that bank account is going on a diet. And not a happy, healthy diet either.

Figure out your freelance finances before you make any changes. Find out how much money you need and start saving up that emergency fund before you quit your job. Once you know your money needs, you'll be better able to plan your freelance transition.

Just don't go blindly jumping into freelance work. Take the time to come up with a freelance transition plan.

Here are some examples of what that freelance transition might look like:

Moonlighting

Perhaps the most popular way to ease into freelancing is by moonlighting. You work your 9-to-5 job and then put on your freelance pants at night. Currently 27% of freelancers[12] work this way (that's more than 14 million people).

It's perfect for the freelance transition because you can build up

---

11   https://ithemes.com/2014/10/28/ready-go-freelance/

12   https://www.freelancersunion.org/blog/
dispatches/2014/09/04/53million/

clients, income and a portfolio, all while still earning a steady paycheck. That extra money can help cover your startup costs or build your emergency fund.

The downside is you're putting in a lot of hours. But no one said the freelance transition was easy.

Part-Time Job

Another approach is to go ahead and quit your 9-to-5 job, but take on a part-time job to help pay the bills. People with multiple sources of income are called diversified workers and they make up 18% of freelancers[13] (or 9 million people). For some this isn't a transition plan, but a constant state.

The part-time job approach to your freelance transition allows you to continue earning a steady income without the demands and stress of a regular 9-to-5 job. Depending on your part-time job, you'll probably have more time and energy to pour into freelancing. You can still build up clients, income and your portfolio until you're ready to move into freelancing full time.

This is a more aggressive dive into freelancing. You'll likely be earning less than your full-time job. That's the potential downside. You might not have as much income to help you build up an emergency fund or cover startup costs.

Turn Your Boss Into a Client

If you're leaving your job on good terms you might be able to turn your old job into a freelance transition.

---

13   https://www.freelancersunion.org/blog/
dispatches/2014/09/04/53million/

If your boss knows you're stepping away, they might be willing to let you do your own job on a freelance basis until they can find someone to replace you.

It could be a win-win—you get to start freelancing with a steady client and your boss gets an easier transition. It could also lead to more clients.

But this approach only works if your employer is on board. If they're not, well, you might have an awkward time keeping your job and trying to moonlight.

Other Freelance Transition Options

There are lots of other ways to transition into freelance. **You could win the lottery.** Or, more realistically, a relative might be willing to help you out with a **no-interest loan** or an **early inheritance**. Just be careful of any loans. That's not free money. You'll need to include loan payments in your expenses.

The No Parachute Method

Another way to plan your freelance transition is to jump without a parachute. **This isn't exactly recommended.** It works best for people with very few expenses and obligations (if you've got kids and loans, you better rethink it).

But there is a certain appeal. If you work best under pressure, this might be good for you. It's high risk, but high reward. **Sometimes you need to take risks.** They force you to do what needs to be done.

That's what Cortez did. He burned the ships to quell mutiny and push his men forward. No going back!

(OK, the ships were scuttled, not burned. Score one for historical accuracy[14]. But the basic idea is sound.)

But it's definitely not for everyone. Most people need some kind of safety net to fall back on.

Freelance Transition Tips

As you think about how you're going to plan your freelance transition, here are a few tips to help you through:

Try It First

As much as we love and support freelancers, it's not for everyone. Not everyone works well being their own boss. Some people crave direction and leadership. It's comforting knowing someone else is worrying about the big picture strategy. That's not a sign of weakness. People are just different. Freelancing is natural for some people. It can make other people squirm.

Before you make the freelance leap, **find ways to try it out and make sure freelancing is for you.** Try a few moonlighting projects, even if you're not planning to moonlight. It's a big shift, so get a taste before you commit.

Don't Burn Your Bridges

Like Cortez, you might find motivation in burning your ships (OK, scuttling), but there's nothing to be gained by burning your bridges (whoa, mixed metaphor headache).

---

14   http://en.wikipedia.org/wiki/Spanish_conquest_of_the_Aztec_ Empire#Scuttling_the_fleet_.26_Aftermath

You may be excited to leave your full-time job, but don't say mean things and slam the door on any potential opportunities. Sometimes that former job will turn into freelance work or your former boss will offer new leads. **Do everything you can to leave on good terms.**

Build Connections

You need to start building relationships as soon as you can. Not just with potential clients, but with other freelancers as well. 81% of freelancers[15] refer work to other freelancers. Start making those connections today.

Go Deeper

As you land your first clients, always look for ways to go deeper with them. Ask questions to see what other problems you can solve for them. You're trying to build a long-term relationship.

And you need to think long term. This isn't milking every client for more work. It's just good service. Get to know your clients and figure out how you can help them. It might not pay off now. **But your clients will remember that you treated them right.** It will pay off down the road.

Soak It Up

As you dive into your freelance transition you're going to realize something quickly: **You've got a lot to learn.**

Put the ego aside and own up to the fact that you don't know it all. Soak up all the knowledge and insight you can get. Learn from others.

---

15   https://www.freelancersunion.org/blog/dispatches/2014/07/01/
freelance-life-survey-report/

You'll have to make some of your own mistakes—that's just part of life—but you want to avoid as many as you can.

Winning the Freelance Transition

Start your freelance career right by making the right transition. It's a big leap, but there can be plenty of rewards. Just don't forget your parachute. We all want you to land safely.

Story: Unemployed

KEVIN D. HENDRICKS, FREELANCE WRITER, MONKEY OUTTA
NOWHERE

If you lose a job and get **severance** and/or
unemployment, that might be a way to transition into
freelance.

That's how it worked for me. When my company
relocated I got a small severance package and was
eligible for unemployment. I'd been looking for a new job,
but I'd also been moonlighting. With my day job gone, I
was pursing more and more of those moonlighting jobs.

At the time unemployment was structured so it could
supplement any income I had coming in. So getting a
part time job wouldn't disqualify me for unemployment.
The program encouraged you to work, but also didn't
consider any job a win. They wanted you to find a
well-paying job similar to what you had. So they didn't
force you to snub your nose at whatever temporary
opportunities came along in order to keep getting
unemployment checks.

Unemployment served as a safety net until I could get
established as a freelancer. Unemployment doesn't
always work that way and it varies by state (plus this
was over a decade ago). I also had a lot going for me in
my situation, including an employment counselor and
available funds for training, which I used to take a small
business class.

It doesn't always work that well, but losing my job worked
as a perfect transition into freelance work.

Story: Leave on Good Terms

BRIAN CASEL, FREELANCE DESIGNER

What tips do you have for beginning freelancers?

My very first clients came as referrals from my former boss at the agency. I left on really great terms. So that's one tip: if you're coming from an agency and going freelance, leave on good terms.

What often happens is the agency works with very large clients. The type of clients I'd work with are too small for an agency to take on budget-wise, so the agency is happy to pass on smaller leads, so that's what happened.

You can start out on job boards. These days there are many more job boards than there were back then. You can get a little traction early on by responding to job boards. Then the network of referrals should kick in if you're doing great work and being reliable—being the guy who delivers on time, delivers quality work and communicates really well. That's worked out pretty well for me.

You'd be amazed—that alone can set you apart quite a bit. There are so many flakes in this business. If you're doing those things you're well ahead of the pack.

Self Evaluation

We've talked about the philosophy and mindset you need to have as a freelancer. You may have noticed that it needs to be inherently different from an office worker who goes in every day to work for someone else and punches out at the end of the day.

Freelancing is different.

You can't go into freelancing like it's just another job.

If all this philosophizing about freelancing resonates with you, then you're on the right track. If it sounds like a bunch of crap, you might need to reevaluate whether or not freelancing is for you. We're not saying you need to buy in to everything we say, but there is a different mentality. At least recognize that.

Now instead of pie in the sky philosophy, let's get practical. **Is this for you?**

We need to talk about why you're going freelance. You need to make sure you understand what you're getting into when you start your own freelance business—and if you can handle it. Freelancing is a big change—it's not like switching jobs or even switching careers. It's a whole lifestyle change. It requires a different way of thinking, a different way of working and a different way of being. You shouldn't make a change like that without some serious thought and self-reflection.

Start With Why

Regardless of what business you are in, in order for it to be successful you have to believe in it and be passionate about it. This is what we mean by "Start With Why".

What is your "why" for going into freelancing? Why are you doing this? What do you hope to gain? Hope to experience? Want to give? Is there a legacy you want to leave?
How will your life, your family life or your part of the world be better because you are doing this work?

Start by identifying your personal *why*.

Tip: A book we highly recommend is *Start With Why: How Great Leaders Inspire Everyone to Take Action* by Simon Sinek. Being a freelancer means knowing how to inspire yourself. Having a strong enough "why" is one way to do that.

Self Exploration

The nuts and bolts of freelancing can wait while you slow down and weigh the pros and cons. Do you really understand what this entails and are you ready for it?

Sit down and ask yourself some serious questions:

- **How well do you work alone?** Freelancing can be a solitary life, and if you're an extrovert who craves personal interaction, that might be hard to swallow. You can always find ways around this, from working at a coffee shop to co-working, but it's an important consideration.

- **How do you drive and motivate yourself?** Being a freelancer means being your own boss. Unfortunately there are no underlings to boss around. It's just you. So you need to be self-motivated. You need to be willing to do what it takes to succeed— whether that's high-powered business meetings or taking out the trash. It's all you. If you need someone standing over you and telling you what to do, you won't get far.

- **Can you meet deadlines?** This one is important. If you can't hit deadlines, it's not going to work. Sometimes free-wheeling creative types have a hard time with deadlines. If that's you, either get serious about deadlines or find another line of work.

- **Are you willing to make sacrifices?** Freelancing is hard work and it will require saying no to other opportunities. There are times when you'll need to miss out on fun things with friends or important family obligations.
  The upside is there are other times when you get to set the priorities. But being a freelancer means you can't just call in sick. It's easy to get distracted and there's nobody to hold you to the grindstone.

- **Can you be organized?** Not every freelancer is super organized.

It's not a must-have requirement, but you need to be organized enough. If you thrive on chaos, you'll have to make a special effort to be organized. Be chaotic in your creative process or in how you keep your desk, but make sure your business files are perfectly organized.

- **Can you work hard without an immediate reward?** Sometimes people think freelancing is an easy way to get rich quickly. It's not. At least not usually. It's hard work and requires consistent effort over time. And sometimes it doesn't pay well, especially in the beginning. You'll have to make sacrifices and it may be years before you make decent money. You need to be willing to put in the time, work hard and wait for your investment to pay off.

- **Is this really something you want to do?** If you're a half-hearted freelancer, you'll completely fail. Your business is really just a hobby in that case. Being a hobbyist is fine, but it leads to failure as a business owner. You need to be passionate about this. No dragging your feet.

Count the Cost
We've talked about the risks and rewards of freelancing. You need to count the cost. Let's look at a few big issues you need to consider:

- **Partner's Thoughts:** If you're married or in a serious relationship, what does your spouse or significant other think? Launching a freelance career is much bigger than switching jobs. It's going to have a big impact on your life and it's likely going to cause some relationship stress.
  If your relationship is truly a partnership, you need to talk it over together.

- **Money in Order:** We talked about the new money mindset you need with freelancing. Are your finances in order? Do you have enough savings to cover times when work is slow?

Have you minimized your personal debt and expenses so you can get by on less?

- **Ready to Work:** Establishing yourself as a freelancer can take a lot of hard work. You need to build trust with new clients and prove that you can deliver. You might have some lean months at the beginning until you can establish yourself. Are you prepared to work through it? Are you ready for long days and late nights?

- **Ready for Frugal:** Those tight months might be a drain on your savings and your time. Are you prepared to put off buying a new, well, anything and make do with what you have?

- **Bye Bye Safety Net:** Leaving a steady job means leaving that safety net of a guaranteed paycheck, good health insurance, a retirement plan, vacation days, etc. Of course nothing is guaranteed in life, but there is a lot more uncertainty as a freelancer. There's also a lot more reward. This will undoubtedly bring some extra stress into your life. Are you prepared to handle it?

Test the Waters

Try freelancing before you make the leap. Test the waters and find out if this is really for you. There's so much about freelancing that's different and you need to get a taste.

You might find that you love it and you're thirsting for more.

You might find a sour taste in your mouth.
Better to know early before you quit your day job or do anything rash.

We talked earlier about ways you can transition to freelancing and try it out before you fully commit. Do it.

It's not only a good way to ease your way into freelancing, but you'll get a sense of whether or not this is truly for you.

Get Advice

This is a big decision, so get some good input.

Seek Advice

Definitely get some advice from other freelancers, business owners and even mentors or business coaches. This is a big decision and you need to get all the input you can. Ask lots of questions, talk about your fears and find out how it worked for them.

Grain of Salt

You may not agree with everything and not all advice is good advice. But iron sharpens iron and it's good to share ideas and get some outside perspective.

You should also ask friends and family for their input. They likely know you the best and can give some helpful insights. But don't weigh their input too heavily; sometimes friends and family can be overly generous with their praise—or worse, overly stingy. They may see your weaknesses as roadblocks instead of just caution signs. So take their advice with a grain of salt.

Mentors

One of the great benefits of mentors and advisors is that you get to learn from their pain and mistakes at a fraction of the cost they paid to go through it.

Your mentors should be seasoned (older than you), with a background of rich and diverse experiences.

Mentors are happy to 'give it all away', with the goal of leaving their legacy imprint upon you.

Mentors are truth tellers. They aren't like your mom who likes everything you do on Facebook (sorry Mom!). They don't sugar coat the truth just to pacify your ego. They simply want the best for you. Mentors help you see your blind spots as they help you get perspective. They are partners for life.

- Sometimes they pick you up.
- Sometimes they pull you back down to reality.
- Sometimes they put their boot in your butt and a fire in your pants.
- Sometimes they walk beside you through the dark and scary times.

Here's how to find a good mentor:

- **Identify, then observe potential mentors:** See how they act when no one is looking. Don't stalk them, just observe how they act toward and around others.

- **Make sure they deserve to be your mentor:** Do they have an ego to be fed by you, or are they looking at multiplying their influence in the world through you? They must first and only want your ultimate best—mentorship is about legacy, not selfish gain or ego.

- **Buy lunch or coffee on their terms:** After you've identified someone you want to potentially be your mentor, seek out the easiest way to speak one-on-one based on their schedule. Don't assume they have time to spend an afternoon with you. Work around their schedule.

- **Start by asking them questions and heed their advice with action:** Show them you are willing to act and move on their advice.

- **Good mentors are teachers who are learners:** You're not looking for educators per se, but people who are actively seeking to get better and willingly sharing it with others. Good mentors pass it on and pay it forward.

- **Again, respect and value their time!**

The last parting thought about mentors is this: One day when you get ahead, commit to be a mentor to someone else who asks.

Story: Mentors
JUSTIN SAINTON, FREELANCE DEVELOPER, ZAO

How did you pick up knowledge—whether it was coding or business—without going to school?

As the WordPress community has grown, one of the most massively helpful things to make up for that lack of formal education is being in the trenches with a bunch of other people doing the same thing, many of whom are further down the road than I am. Being able to glean from others, like Cory Miller at iThemes, Chris Lema and others—that's way more valuable to me than any kind of schooling.

So find a mentor. Find someone who is where you want to be in 10 years. Buy them coffee, take them out to lunch, ask for their counsel. Ask them to look at the way you're doing it and give you advice. I have several people who I consider mentors. The only reason I never went to school is because I've had mentors who have provided that counsel and I've benefited from their experience. It's been invaluable.

Go!

We've talked about the philosophy of freelancing—the mindset you need to get your head around.

We've asked some hard questions and hopefully you've done the work of self-evaluation. (If you haven't done it, do it. Take the time to think through those questions. Skipping them is only cheating yourself.)

We've talked about how to make that transition and the friends you'll need along the way.

We've talked about the value of outside advice and hopefully you've talked to some people who can give you insight and direction.

Now it's the moment of decision: **Is freelancing for you?**

Hopefully you're firm and confident in your answer. For many of you it was never really in question. That's OK. Before launching into a new endeavor like this it's important to slow down and reflect. Look before you leap. For others this is a journey and you're still figuring out the destination. It's important to work through these questions and be firm in your decision.

From here on out we'll dive into the practical realities of freelancing.

But we believe it's important to have the right foundation, to understand what you're getting into and realize the impact it has on your life and those around you. You need to have your head in the right place.

If you're still unsure about freelancing, spend some more time thinking and sorting it out. Maybe keep reading so you can further soak in the ideas and realities of what this journey is about. Then come back and re-evaluate.

And if you're ready… let's go.

Organization

Going to work as a freelancer is not some hobby. This is serious business. If you want to succeed, you need to plan for it. Otherwise expect to fail.

25-year freelance veteran Ryan Oakes says[16]:

"I believe you are a business the moment you begin to even freelance. You are in business with yourself, and consequently, that business needs a business plan."

We're not talking about moonlighters looking to bank some extra income and pay off loans or swing a better vacation. They can wing it and if they fail there's always the day job. No harm, no foul.

But if you're going to be a full-time freelancer, then a freelance business plan is a must.

So in this section we're offering a simple blueprint to drafting a business plan for your freelance business.

---

16   https://www.freelancersunion.org/blog/2014/02/13/planning-growth-it-starts-day-one/

More than a fill-in-the-blanks business plan template, this is more a series of topics, common themes and questions you'll need to wrestle with (and you'll keep wrestling with as your business grows).

We strongly recommend you actually write a business plan. For many of you it will be required, especially if you need to convince family or secure a loan. But that doesn't mean your business plan needs to be boring. It's a living document and it will grow with you.

This section is meant to be a primer for getting started in the right direction. We've tried to be as comprehensive as possible, though your mileage may vary.

But don't get overwhelmed.

Complete as much as you can now, then come back and flesh out other stuff later.

Plans can and do change. This is your first draft that you'll consistently hone and perfect over time and experience. You are always testing ideas and concepts to see which ones work and help you sustain your business for the long term.

Some of your ideas will fail—miserably. When you find success it might look drastically different from what you envisioned in your business plan. You have to evolve and adapt. That's how business works.

You might get a first draft done, then not return for a year or more. Or you could continually tweak it from month to month as your business grows and you learn what works and what doesn't.

Sometimes your idea of the perfect client will make you miserable. And so you'll fire those clients. Do so, and move on.

Learn as you go. This "business plan" is truly a work in progress.

Story: I Hate Business Plans

CORY MILLER, FOUNDER, ITHEMES

I have a confession: I hate traditional business plans. Too often they become academic (and unrealistic) exercises and don't turn into real action. Many people think they should be 100-plus pages, contain every possible situation and scenario, and be a final product. In fact, they aren't. And most businesses can't be dreamed up in a vacuum. The initial idea or concept must be tested, refined, tested and refined some more.

My "business plan" for my freelance business was initially just to keep doing work I enjoyed and making money at it to pay off some bills. At some point though, my profitable hobby got serious. So I needed to formalize what I was doing.

My initial "business plan" for iThemes was simple: make money selling WordPress themes full time. I didn't have a super polished presentation. In fact, the paperwork to setup iThemes Media LLC as a legal entity was and probably still is the most slick document we have.

But I did keep a simple text document with ideas, plans, strategies, tactics, and a list of items to do and accomplish. It was more of a living document and it changed often as we started the business and found what actually works and what doesn't.

My experience isn't a license to slack off on your business plan. Getting serious about freelancing and organizing your strategies is important. But find a way to do it that works for you. If that's an academic, textbook approach, great. If that's more of a scattered, organized chaos approach, do it.

Nuts & Bolts

More than anything, the purpose of a freelance business plan is to force you to answer all the appropriate **questions about running** a business. It's to make sure you're not taking any shortcuts.

Don't think of a business plan as a burden. It's not one more thing on your plate. It's the core of what you do. It's putting down on paper exactly how you're going to make ends meet. You can't just say you'll do work and people will pay you. You need to write out a plan for how you'll make money.

A business plan covers everything. It's one of these catch-all, far-reaching documents that answers all questions, covers all contingencies and tells you where to go and how to get there. It will answer realistic questions about whether or not you'll have enough money to buy a computer or how much you need to be charging. It can be pretty overwhelming to write, but it will help you immensely.

These are questions you have to answer, or you have no business trying to freelance.

Writing a business plan is the kind of stodgy thing they teach in business classes, so if you steered clear of anything so practical in college, it might be time to hit the books.

But a business plan doesn't have to be boring. You can put your creativity to work as you design your business plan, so that it is a reflection of you and the business you want to create. Just make sure you address everything that needs addressing.

Different schools of thought will tell you different things to include. In general your business plan should cover your company's vision, goals, marketing plan, some market research and some numbers (we'll go deeper into this later, but include things like your expenses, your expected income, how much you need to break even, etc.).

You'll need to think through things like how many jobs you'll need to do in a year to pay your bills and keep yourself fed. It's very specific stuff that may seem hard at first (that's the point), but you really have to think it through.

This is a good time to do market research and think about what kind of freelancer you're going to be. How are you going to stand out from the crowd? There are lots of developers and designers out there and they're all competing for the same bucks you are. What makes you different? We'll talk more about branding later, but make sure you put it in your business plan.

Don't Run Screaming

We're not talking about a stuffy business plan with legalese, hundreds of pages and weird spreadsheets no one understands. **Don't be scared away by overdone business plans.**

Your freelance business plan is for you. It's a document to help you make money. **It shouldn't be something to fear, it should be your friend.**

Unless you need to get investors on board or convince a bank to give you a loan, **it's likely no one will even see your freelance business plan but you.**

Now you could use that as an excuse to blow it off. But you'll only be hurting yourself.

Instead, the fact that no one needs to see it should be a relief. There's no pressure here. The whole point is to focus on how you're going to make money, laying out the details and making sure everything makes sense. It's not supposed to be homework. You shouldn't worry about someone correcting it. You should worry about making it useful.

It's your plan. Make it your own.

Goals & Objectives

What do you want to accomplish? Here are some questions to get you started:

1. What do you want and need from the business?

This is about your work, life and financial goals. Most freelancers and entrepreneurs want freedom and flexibility over their work life. Think about what motivates you, inspires you, the work you enjoy doing and what it all means for your life and family.

2. What do you want your work life to be and look like?

Make a sustainable living doing enjoyable work on your terms and with people you enjoy.

3. What are you financial needs and desires?

What is the break even number needed to pay your bills? (It's important to factor in quarterly taxes particularly if you're living in the U.S.)

4. What do you need to do to make all this happen?

Use your break even number to determine how many clients you need.

Remember: How do you eat an elephant? One bite at a time. Break it down into manageable, realistic action steps and goals.

Story: Jared Atchison

JARED ATCHISON, FREELANCE DEVELOPER

What was the catalyst that pushed you into full-time freelance WordPress development?

I would say one thing that had the biggest impact was going to my first WordCamp, which was WordCamp Houston (RIP) in August 2010.

At that point I had been using WordPress for over a year for clients (working for Texas A&M). I was starting to get rather obsessed. I watched the wp-hackers mailing list like a hawk. I constantly monitored and helped out in the #wordpress IRC chat room. I read all the WordPress news sites (back then, there were only two or three). I followed all the known WordPress developers on Twitter. I wouldn't have called myself a WordPress expert, but my skill level was above average.

Then I attended WordCamp Houston, and the speakers blew me away. I couldn't believe what I saw. In front of me were many people who did almost exactly what I did, except they had their own business. They made a living, independently, using WordPress to help out their clients.

At that point, I knew my growing obsession with WordPress, would some day pay off. At that moment, I didn't know how long it would take, but I knew one day I was going to be one of these people who had their own business anchored around WordPress. I'd be one of these people who presented sessions and young developers looked up to.

How did you break through and become successful? What strategies or approaches seemed to work the best?

Making a game plan and then following through with the execution.

After attending WordCamp in Houston, I got home and started pondering what to do next. I needed a plan of attack. I couldn't just go quit my job and say, "Great, now I'm a WordPress freelancer." That would be a quick way to rejoin the corporate world. I needed to think things through and be patient, which admittedly wasn't always easy.

So I came up with a plan that had a few objectives (with some overlap between them).

First, hone my skill. I wanted to become a WordPress "expert," much like some of the people I saw speak at WordCamp. I was already very familiar with WordPress and technically savvy, but I knew that wouldn't be enough. I wanted to be a top-tier developer. If I'm going to swing, swing for the fences.

So I put in a ton of work and immersed myself with WordPress. I spent time sharpening my developer skills. I didn't want to be a snake oil developer and I don't really buy into "fake it until you make it." Instead I wanted legitimately to be able to provide my future clients with a good value.

Secondly, build my brand. As I got my skill as a developer up to my high standards, the next move was to start building some sort of brand for myself. I couldn't create and launch my own successful business without a brand. This was a slow process, and was actually harder, in my opinion, than learning the development.

I also think this is often where many freelancers mess up. You can have all the technical skill in the world, but without a brand to support it, you won't succeed with your own business. Having grown up with parents running a family business I knew that had to be incorporated into my game plan.

Lastly was the transition. While I was expanding my skills and building up my brand, I was still working full time at my day job. Eventually, when the time was right, I had to plan out a transition.

And that's exactly what I did. At first I was just moonlighting and working extra hours. I'd come home in the evenings and then spend three to five hours doing side freelance work. Wow, was that a grind, but I knew it would get worse before it got better.

After doing that for a while I had enough work where I was able to go half time at my day job. Then, eventually, I was able to quit completely. I'll never forget how I felt the day I went to work for myself and didn't have a day job—liberating. For me, I didn't think just quitting my day job, and be forced to "sink or swim" was a good (or responsible) option, so I eased into it. It wasn't easy, but in the end I think it was the right way.

What keeps you successful as a WordPress freelancer?

Being stubborn and developing a systematic approach to business.

There are WordPress developers out there who do things I can barely comprehend. I see it on GitHub all the time. There are also people who are naturally gifted at running a business. Who cares? I don't let that stop me.

My first year running my own business, there were a lot of mistakes. Damn, were there mistakes. Initially I just wasn't great at managing the business. I let clients boss me around. I couldn't keep a straight schedule (in part thanks to clients bossing me around). However, I kept going. I was stubborn.

The important thing is to learn from your mistakes and put systems in place to prevent it from happening again. In college I didn't consider myself a systematic person, far from it. However, developing that attribute I think has been important to my business being successful.

Again, being from a family of business owners, I know that running your own business isn't always easy. There are a lot of challenges, especially for the greenhorns. I think I was lucky that I had realistic expectations, and I was determined to keep my head down and move forward.

Lastly, I always try to put myself in a position to learn new things. I don't ever want to get complacent. This applies to not just the technical side of things, but also running my business.

Products & Services

You need to think through the services you're going to offer:

1. What are you most passionate about and enjoy doing?

Doing something just because you think it'll make money isn't a long-term plan. You need to actually enjoy doing the work at least for a time before you can hire someone else to do it.

2. What do you want to offer?

List all the types of things you'll offer such as: web design services (WordPress theme design, mobile/responsive sites, ecommerce, blogging design, plugin development, BuddyPress, membership sites, etc.), marketing (email and social media marketing), support and maintenance, retainers, content creation, products (WordPress themes, ebooks, membership programs), hosting, etc.

3. What results and outcomes does it provide clients?

This is more higher-level thinking and positioning, but it's an important step to a sustainable business model. If you know what you're truly offering your clients you can better sell it. Are you helping them get their organizations on the web, taking it to the next level, increasing their brand exposure and customer base, increasing revenue (like helping them sell their products online) or reaching new customers?

4. How is it unique or better than what's out there?

How are you different from your competition?

5. What is the right price to sustain business and get clients?

Will you charge hourly or per projects? For rookies, it's helpful to start with hourly and once you start to understand how fast you are and how long projects take then you can slowly start to switch to project-based billing.

6. Can you deliver it?

Do you have the skills, time and commitment to deliver to clients? If not, scale back, and start learning how now.

7. What is your efficient process for delivering it?

Time is money. Figure out how you can deliver fast with quality so you can charge more for your quality services or take on more clients.

8. What ancillary services can you offer to support your income?

Are there services or products around what you do that can help you make more money while providing great service to your clients? You may stumble onto these while serving your clients and hearing/sensing their needs.

These aren't primary revenue generators for you. They just add to your income without taking a ton of your time or energy.

Clients

You need to define your clients. Here are some questions that can help:

1. Who do you want to serve?

Think of all the people you know who are potential clients. If you've been doing work part time, who were your favorite people to work with? This gets to the core of finding your "ideal" or "perfect" client.

2. How specific can you get?

If your perfect client is too general, you'll never be able to reach them. You can't serve everybody. You need to narrow your focus and zero in on a very specific niche.

3. Are they easily identifiable?

The easier it is to identify clients, the easier it is to target them with marketing (which we'll work through in a separate section). Do you already have them in your contact book? Or access to them and know what they look like? List as much as you can about them.

4. Are they relatively easy to reach?

List where they congregate in person or online, what they read, etc.

5. What are they looking for?

List their biggest needs, wants, hassles, struggles, obstacles for getting their organizations online.

6. What niches, industries or types of people can you identify?

List all of these you've worked in, for or have experience with. It might help to look at your resume for trends.

7. Do you have contacts in the field? Or experience with them?
Mine your social profiles and connections on Facebook, LinkedIn, Twitter, etc., in addition to your resume, email, phone, etc. List them all and in particular highlight the influencers you know.

Marketing
Once you define those clients, how will you reach them?

1. How do you reach your ideal clients?
We talked about clients that are easily identifiable and reachable. Now you're drilling down specifically with the start of a plan to get the message about your services and its benefits in front of them.

What influencers will you contact first to let them know what you're doing? What magazines or blogs do they read where you can write guest posts?

2. What educational content can you offer to attract your ideal client?
Could you start a blog, write an ebook or whitepaper, or do guest posts on other blogs or niche websites?

3. How much will it cost you?
It's not just money. It's also time, energy and resources, too, each day and week.

4. How many clients do you need to sustain your business?
This is where you'll need to do some math. Take that break even number and start breaking it into projects and clients and estimate how much work you think you'll need.

Here's a tip: You'll probably need more than you think. Expenses come up and clients flake out. Be prepared.

5. How do you generate leads?

Leads are people interested in your work. But they don't always turn into clients. So you need to maximize the amount of leads in your business.

Who are the first set of leads you can contact who are likely to turn into your first clients? How can you continue to generate leads each week? And how will you ultimately turn them into paying clients? What support material will you need to convince them?

Don't worry. Often, you won't know this until you get your first set of leads. Consistently doing good work for others will quickly become your biggest asset. People talk well of those who do good work and deliver on their promises.

Additionally, a good portfolio of work helps sell those leads on your services. Design sells. Thus links on your client sites can help drum up more work for you.

6. How do you present your value proposition to potential clients?

You need be able to clearly present what you do and how you can help your prospective clients in their work.

Post what you do and the benefits for clients clearly on your website. Do a slide deck and post on SlideShare (then it'll be ready for an in-person or online client presentation later).

The best way to hone a presentation is to give it to a real prospective client.

Who can be your first test subject?

7. How do you show off your best work?

You want to be able to share your work with others easily—whether that's through a portfolio section on your website, Dribbble.com, social media, etc.

You need an easy-to-update and easy-to-share method of displaying your latest and greatest work.

Story: Bill Erickson

BILL ERICKSON, FREELANCE DEVELOPER

How did you first get into WordPress?

I got started in WordPress in 2005. I was a freshman in college studying business and interested in web design. Our business honors group was hiring a web designer—I thought, "I could do that."

My job was to update the content. They'd copy and paste text from the website, make one or two changes and email it back to me. Instead of spending hours and hours making text changes, I wanted to build it so they could manage it themselves.

So I played with WordPress and it worked really well. We started using WordPress for other sites at the university. It was just a matter of making it so the content editors could edit content instead of going through the developers.

I was a finance major when the finance world collapsed, so I could go after a nonexistent job or go freelance. So I've been doing that ever since.

Did you start freelancing right out of college?

Working for the university, I was a student worker making $10 per hour. So for my first freelance project I didn't know how to quote a price, so I just worked for $10 per hour. I spent a long time working and not making any money.

One thing that really helped me get started was that I had minimal expenses. My goal was to make $2,000 per month. Back then I thought if I could make that much it'd be amazing. A lot of freelancers can understand this—having those lower expenses you're able to succeed faster and grow your business from there.

It would have been much harder if I had a corporate job and then tried to get into freelancing. I took four to five years to figure things out, build a name for myself and charge a premium for my services. I could experiment without having a ton of bills to pay.

What prompted you to start doing WordPress as a freelancer?

Recognizing the need. Once I built WordPress sites for a few people, I realized how many people want it. Everyone needs a website. There weren't many great solutions out there, so there was a ton of demand from businesses. I've built sites for people and it's replaced a $1,000 per month retainer they were paying. The client is able to take control of their business. By lowering costs, they can do more.

After I did a few WordPress sites, I realized this huge market opportunity. That's still the case. Every good developer is booked for months and there's way more work than there are quality developers.

Finances

Let's talk money.

1. How do you properly manage finances?
Managing your cash flow is vital to your continued success. Without cash, your business is dead. A good experienced accountant is a key partner to help you navigate taxes and provide good financial management.

2. How and when do you get paid?
Ensuring you are getting paid on a timely basis is key (cash flow is oxygen). Do you get a 50% deposit upfront and 50% on delivery, which is typical in web design? Are you paid via PayPal or via check?

3. How do you pay others & taxes?
This is where your accountant can help. In the U.S., welcome to quarterly taxes as a business owner.

4. What are your expenses?
This is for your personal and business finances. What is your monthly minimum burn rate? The minimum amount of cash you need to pay your bills and eat. What can you cut to make your burn rate as low as possible?

5. How much cash cushion do you need to go full time?

Before you go full time with your business, you'll want a savings cushion for the feast or famine times of freelancing. Typically, you'll want to save several months of your monthly burn rate. Some people do three months, six months or over a year. It's up to you and your family and what you ultimately feel comfortable and confident with.

6. What essential starter investments do you need to make for the business?

Do you need a new computer, any software, or other tools like hosting or WordPress products? You'll often start with the bare minimum and upgrade as you go. We'll talk more about specific toys and tools you need later, but you need to include them in your business plan.

Legal

Lawyer Up

If you've decided to freelance then it's time to get serious. As serious as a lawyer. One of the first things you should do is protect yourself legally by setting up a separate business entity. Maybe you'll be an S-Corp or an LLC—ask a lawyer for the details. But you need to do this.

Setting up a separate business entity is an important legal step to protect your personal assets. It puts a legal buffer between your company and yourself. It's a way to protect yourself and your family.

Let's say you start a business and neglect to incorporate. Or maybe you decide you'll just do it later. Either way, six months down the road you have a client who seemed nice, but they don't like your work and it gets ugly. They decide to sue, and suddenly they're going after your personal assets. Your house, your savings, your retirement are all in jeopardy.

But if you had a business entity then this sour client could only sue for your company assets and cash. They couldn't go after your personal savings.

And don't say it'll never happen to you. Because that's when it happens to you.

Tip: Hire a lawyer and get some expert legal advice on this. It's worth the money. Laws vary by country and state, so you need to do your research and talk to an expert. Depending on your needs and your own expertise you might be able to do some of this yourself. But still get that expert opinion so you know you're making the right decision, even if you decide to do the paperwork yourself.

How Do You Structure Your Business and Keep It Legal?

Your business plan needs to cover all these legal issues and give you a plan to keep things on the up and up.

1. How will you structure your business to get started?
Limited Liability Corporations are often the most popular, easiest way for freelancers to structure their businesses in the U.S. But this is why a business attorney is a key initial partner for you. A capable, experienced attorney will help you navigate the legal structure.

2. What contracts or agreements will I need?
Many freelancers have client contracts that they insist on signing before work begins. Generally speaking, the bigger the money and client involved, the more necessary agreements become. However, that is why you should talk with an attorney.

3. How do you get ongoing legal help when you need it?
Again, it's good to have access as needed to a business attorney to bounce things off or to assist and advise with the creation of agreements.

I remember getting a 15-page legal contract one time and was frightened by the language (and for good reason). One of my partners is also an attorney and his help has been invaluable.

People & Partners
Whose help do you need?

1. What "big picture" help do you need?
Hopefully throughout this chapter you're identifying areas you'll need help with (and yes, you should need help). The top three partners for any business endeavor are: Your significant other, accountant and lawyer.

2. What kind of day-to-day help do you need?
Depending on what work you're doing, you might need to bring in other people to help, whether they're partners you're working with or subcontractors you hire, mentors and advisors or even employees. These people are important, so you need to include them in your business plan. You may be going solo, but you're never truly on your own.

Tools
What resources do you need to do it all?

Like people, you'll also identify tools you need to invest in for your business, however small they are. What investments do you need to make in terms of software, training and the like to keep up to date in your business but also on the cutting edge?

Here are some example areas to consider:

- **Accounting Software** - You need a way to track your business finances like income, invoices, taxes, payroll (if you have them). The de facto is QuickBooks. Freshbooks can handle invoicing, and PayPal or Stripe are good for online payments.

- **Client/Project Management** - How are you going to communicate with clients and keep up with tasks/milestones for your projects? For email, check out Gmail for Domains. Try Basecamp or Trello for project management.

- **Computer/Software** - Macbook Air, Google Chrome, Google Talk, Paypal and iPhone might be your favorites to keep everything going efficiently and effectively. Figure out whatever toys you need.

- **Continuing Education/Training** - What kind of continuing education do you need to stay connected with your field and on top of your game? You might need to attend conferences or check out training courses.

We'll talk more specifics in the Finances chapter. But your business plan needs to consider all the nitty gritty details. Don't just assume you have a computer, so you're set. You'll need to replace that computer one day, right? Your business plan should account for the cost of a new computer every so often (how often is up to you).

Action Steps

What are your next action steps?

Now that you've come this far and completed as much as you can, here are some questions for refinement and next steps.

The most important thing about a plan is executing it. Take that first step, then the next step and the one after. Test and refine your business concepts to see what is sustainable long term.

So with that in mind:

1. What areas do you need help with or need to refine?
Many web designers have trouble with marketing or client development. Be honest about your shortcomings and address them. Ignoring them will only cause problems.

2. What are you stuck on and how can you get past it?
Find ways to overcome those obstacles. Maybe you need to talk to a mentor or a business coach. Sometimes you need experience and outside, unbiased opinions.

3. What's the one thing you can do now to make the biggest impact and progress?
We can easily drown in details, especially in an exercise like this. So step back now and think, what is going to make the biggest impact? What next steps can you take that will give you the biggest bang for your buck? Progress will build momentum.

Now go!

Be Flexible
Remember that your freelance business plan is a living document. **Your business plan can and should change.** It will grow over time. You'll make tweaks. You'll cross sections out and need to rework them.

That's a good thing.

If you're going to be a successful freelancer, you need to be agile. You need to be able to tweak your plan, shift with the times and keep going. Being flexible with your plan is important.

Note: That's not an excuse for skipping the plan.

"It's going to change anyway, so why write it?" is a horrible perspective. You write the freelance business plan now so you have somewhere to change from. You need to know where you're coming from so you can get to where you need to be.

Ultimately, your freelance business plan is an **experiment**. Any good business is. **You'll need to test your plan.** Figure out where it fails and make it better. Nothing is perfect the first time.

Especially in the online world, things change—and change quickly. Social media has sprung up in the past five years and is a force to be reckoned with. YouTube was just getting started in 2006 and now online video is ubiquitous. Blogging isn't even that old in the scheme of things.

The tech world changes quickly, so be prepared to adapt. Rather than being rigid, a solid organizational structure should give you the flexibility to change as needed.

Finally: **Don't stuff your freelance business plan in a manila folder, file it away and forget it.** It's your battle plan. Use it. Tweak it. Refine it.

Finances

You're going to need to look at some hard numbers in order to make freelancing work for you. If math isn't your thing, hire an accountant. You'll be glad you did.

How Much Do You Need?

The biggest question to figure out is how much money you need. That's the million-dollar question (and hopefully not how much you need).

The foundation of your freelance finances is figuring how much money you need to survive. You'll need to come up with a baseline number that's the minimum you need to get by. This will include your own salary (so how much do you really need to live on?), all freelance expenses (office, computer, cell phone, etc.), retirement, insurance, a little cushion so you're not cutting things too close and don't forget taxes.

There's a lot to consider for your freelance finances.

Expenses

We'll start with your expenses. What do you need to buy for your business? This should be a no-brainer, but sometimes people fly right by their expenses and don't take the time to count the cost of running a business. This is a must.

This can be a long list, so you'll need to be thorough and think of everything. This isn't an exhaustive list, but it's a start:

- Computers, software, equipment
- Ongoing education and training (Don't forget this one!)
- Office space, supplies, furniture
- Phones, cell phone, Internet access, utilities
- Healthcare, retirement, savings
- Services: Online tools, accountant, lawyer
- Business expenses: Mileage, marketing costs, business cards, bank fees, etc.
- Salary (you need to pay yourself)
- Taxes

- Give yourself a cushion—there will be times when money doesn't come in and you need to be charging enough to cover those times.

And that's just to get you started. There's a lot you have to pay for when you're on your own. Freelance finances aren't simple.

If it sounds like there's a lot to consider, there is. **In general you'll find that you need to charge more than you think you will.** Thankfully clients are often willing to pay more than you think they will.

Cutting Expenses

When talking about expenses you also need to figure out how to keep them as low as possible. The lower your overhead, the easier it is to turn a profit.

Spending Less

The easiest way to make your freelance finances work is to spend less money. That sounds obvious, and it is, but it's harder to do in practice. Do you really need the super swanky office? Can you make your computer last another year? Do you need to attend that many conferences every year?

You want to have a startup mentality and keep things cheap. Amazon used cheap doors as desks to save money when they first started. Those kinds of strategies can help your company keep the expenses in check.

But it's not just your business expenses. You also need to look at your personal expenses. If you're living life large then your salary will need to match. But if you can find ways to cut your personal expenses and survive on less, then your freelance finances start looking a lot better too.

This might be where some people get confused. Aren't you going freelance so you can make more money? Maybe. You might end up making more money, but you might not. Especially in the beginning.

But the surest way to fail is to assume you'll make more money, live like you will, and force your freelance finances to deliver. With those high-income demands, your business has no room for error. The slightest financial problem will ruin you. But if you cut your expenses, tighten the belt and prepare for some lean living, then you have more margin. If things get ugly, you'll be able to survive. But if they go well, you'll have room to boost your spending without worrying about jeopardizing your business.

Minimize Debt

In many ways the key to making your freelance finances work is to minimize your obligations. What do you have to pay for every month? What are the bills you absolutely must pay? The Internet bill and your mortgage are probably pretty crucial, but going out to eat all the time or going to the movies probably isn't something you have to do. Those are choices you can make every month and adjust as needed, but something like a car payment is debt you're locked into. Reducing those non-essential expenses gives you more freedom.

Nothing takes away your financial freedom like debt. Talk about obligations! Every debt you owe is money you must come up with every month. The more you can minimize business and personal debt, the fewer obligations you'll have and the more room you'll have to make your freelance finances work.

In the end, **it's always easier to spend less than it is to earn more.**

What About Benefits?

Your bills and debts aren't the end of your expenses. Your freelance finances also need to include your benefits.

One of the downsides of leaving the corporate world is that you miss out on benefits:

- Retirement
- Insurance (health, dental, life, disability)
- Vacation/sick time

These are all things you're going to have to pay for yourself. Maybe you'll get lucky and can be covered by your spouse's health insurance. Though in some cases employers aren't pitching in much for family health insurance. Your spouse's coverage might be mostly paid for, but adding you or the kids might be prohibitively expensive.

Chances are you're going to get sick at some point. There will be days when you can't work, and that likely means you're not making any money. You'll need to include that in your freelance finances.

You're also going to need some time off. But that two-week vacation suddenly costs you more than plane tickets and a hotel. It's two weeks with no income.

Be sure to include all these extras in your expenses.

Death & Taxes

Another guaranteed expense you need to plan for is taxes. At that cushy corporate job you were paying FICA and other income tax in every paycheck, through your withholdings.

But there are no withholdings on freelance income. **You need to set aside money yourself to pay your taxes.**
Otherwise you'll be facing an ugly tax bill.

In most cases you'll need to pay your taxes quarterly with estimated payments. If you don't pay enough along the way, you could be looking at penalties when you file your taxes by April 15.

This is where talking to a tax professional can be worth your money. Tax software may be easier on the budget, but it might not help with estimated payments or what qualifies as a business expense.

Story: Budgeting & Debt
CURTIS MCHALE, FREELANCE DEVELOPER

I hate budgeting. I would not budget if it were not for my wife. I understand it's useful and I still do not enjoy it. But it's something you really should do if you want to run a viable business.

When I write about pricing I get lots of hits, but when I write about budgeting and paying off debt, I get way less. I have no debt outside of my mortgage, so my expenses are super low. A couple bad months means I can cut what my normal salary would be in half and still get all the food we need, have a house, etc. If you have lots of debt, you have to make so much more.

I talked to one freelancer who spend all his profit for one year on conferences. He couldn't keep his expenses in check. The problem is never not earning enough. The problem is spending too much. You can never out-earn your spending, it will always catch up to you.

There were certainly times during the first two years when I didn't save enough. I got a big check and would go buy a computer. Not because I needed one, but because I wanted one. One year I didn't save enough for taxes, so I owed $9,000. Taxes are going to happen, so if you pretend they're not or you don't save for them, you're setting yourself up to
owe the government.

Income

All those expenses can be kind of depressing. **Going into business costs a lot of money.** So let's talk about something a little more encouraging: income.

How much do you need to earn to cover all those expenses?

That's the money question, so to speak. This is where you need to figure out how much money you can realistically bring in.

We talked expenses first because you need a realistic baseline and something to shoot for. Maybe you'll find that your expenses are low and you'll have no problem bringing in more than enough income. Or maybe you'll discover that you're planning to spend too much and that's making your income a real challenge. If that's the case, it's time to look closer at your expenses and see if you can bring them down. Otherwise, if your freelance finances aren't making sense, you might need to reconsider freelancing.

A few tips on figuring out your income:

- **Feast or Famine** – Freelance work is known for the feast or famine cycle. Sometimes you have more work than you can handle, other times you're struggling to stay busy. Don't expect your income to be steady. Look for ways to make your income more dependable. Later we'll talk about different strategies to generate recurring revenue.

- **Be realistic** – Don't overestimate. It's far better to underestimate your income than to overestimate. One means you have extra cash to celebrate, the other means you're out of business.

- **Passive income** – The bulk of your income may come from building websites, but don't forget passive sources of income like affiliate fees. Every website you build needs hosting, and that could be affiliate income in your pocket.

There's a lot more that goes into your income—such as how much you charge, when you get paid, etc.—and we'll cover it in the next chapter. But this should get you started thinking about your income.

Startup Money

How much money do you need to start freelancing? When calculating your expenses, hopefully you noticed they were front-loaded. There are a lot of things you have to pay for up front, such as office equipment, computers, lawyer fees and more. Maybe you can find ways to bootstrap those expenses, but the other challenge is your income is likely to be lower when you're first starting out.

Why do you think so many startups began in the garage?

You might need extra money to help with the initial transition to freelance work. This might be a good reason to moonlight first and build up your income before going full time.

We talked about different ways to transition into freelancing earlier and this might have a big impact on how you do it.

Story: How to Grow

BILL ERICKSON, FREELANCE DEVELOPER

You've talked about keeping your business intentionally small—how do you define success for yourself?

When it comes down to it, businesses usually want to grow. If you're making x dollars, your goal for next year is x + y. There are a few ways to approach that. One is to grow your team. You only have 40 hours to work, but if you hire another person, you have 80 hours. The problem is you're increasing your expenses. When growing from one to two people, your expenses go up way more: payroll, HR things, health insurance, taxes, etc.—more business stuff is required. The more employees you have, the lower the marginal cost for that employee, but when you're small each employee does cost a lot.

There are alternatives. By staying a one-person shop, I'm able to move more quickly with the market. If I hired a bunch of specialized developers, what happens if the market changes? Hiring more people grounds you and makes you less mobile. It increases your monthly cost and you take on projects you otherwise wouldn't.

I grow my business in other ways, like efficiency. Analytics is helpful here. It tells me the projects I can make more money on, so I push in that direction.

I make more money through added value, by becoming a brand name online. Some clients want a site for $800 and I'm not a good fit. Other clients care about quality and will pay what it costs. They'll usually research and find me.

By building your name and brand you can charge a premium for higher quality.

Another aspect is making the same money in less time. By being more efficient, I can spend less time and make the same salary. Those are a few ways I grow my business.

Something I have not pursued is offering products. Thomas Griffin is the perfect example of how to do it. I'm not as good of a marketing/sales guy and I hate doing support, but if you can do it, it's great.

A lot of people don't actually run the numbers to see if it's a good business before jumping in. They like the idea of mailbox money—money that comes in with no work—but they don't see the tradeoffs: three months actually creating the product with no money coming in. They also discount the amount of support required. Do an analysis and see if it's worth it before you switch to a product.

Emergency Money

The other expense you need to consider is emergencies. What happens if a client drops you and you've got no income? At your corporate job you had that handy salary coming in every two weeks and life was simple. If things did get ugly and you were let go, there was always unemployment. No such safety net in freelancing.

As a freelancer you have to create your own safety net.

You never know what's going to happen. Some corporate clients will take 90 days to pay you. They're not being mean, that's just their standard practice. Can you wait three months for your income?

It's also possible you'll run into bad clients who don't pay at all. Jobs can go south and sometimes you're better off walking away without any money.

Or it could be unexpected expenses. What happens if your computer crashes? It's not like you can wait until you save up money for a new computer. You need a computer to work.

The unplanned realities of life make an emergency fund a necessity for every freelancer.

Everybody—whether you're a freelancer or not—should have an emergency fund. **But for freelancers that emergency fund needs to be bigger.**

Saving up six to 12 months of income is the standard recommendation. Give yourself plenty of wiggle room. If your expenses are flexible and you can rein things in when income goes south, maybe you can get by with less in your emergency fund.

But think through how much you'll need. Hopefully you won't need it. But you never know—that's why it's an emergency fund. Emergencies happen.

Build Up to a Full Emergency Fund

Saving up half or all of your annual salary might be daunting task. That's a lot of money to stash away. You might not get there right away.

Consider starting off with a smaller emergency fund (maybe three months?) and a plan to stash away the rest. You need some kind of safety net to get started, but you can make it bigger as you go.

Just don't put off building up that emergency fund.

You Need a System

Figuring out your money is complicated.

This is the less-than-glamorous side of freelancing. But it's something you have to do. So figure out how to do it well.

Get an Accountant

A big first step is to talk to an accountant. You probably won't need an accountant on an on-going basis, but you should talk to a professional to get your freelance finances set up properly.

An accountant can talk to you about taxes and retirement plans, which business expenses you can write off and what kind of records you need to keep.

Create a System

Then you need to put a system in place to keep your freelance finances in check.

- Put aside money for taxes and set reminders to make your estimated payments.
- Track and anticipate your income.
- Record your expenses and make sure you're staying within your budget.

Test and See

Even after you calculate everything carefully, you may find out that you're wrong. Test your numbers for your first few months and adjust as needed. Did your expenses come out like you expected or do you need to spend less? Are jobs taking you as long as expected or do you need to set aside (and charge for) more time?

Keep careful notes and adjust your numbers as you go.

Even when you're up and running successfully, you should reevaluate your finances on a regular basis. Your expenses might be steadily rising and you need to make a change. Or maybe it's time to start charging more (cha-ching!).

Mechanics

You know how to design a website, but how does freelancing actually work? The mechanics of freelancing can often mess up beginners:

What do you charge?

How do you get paid?

How do you close a deal?

You'll need to get your head around these basics, whether it's pricing or contracts.

What Should I Charge?

One of the first things you need to figure out—and the most common question for new freelancers—is what should you charge? It's an important question, unfortunately there's no simple answer. In order to figure it out you need to do a lot of work, ask some important questions and even do some trial and error. Arriving at your freelance rate is not a simple calculation, but it is very important to your success.

There are three major things you can base your rate on:

- Experience
- Knowledge
- Confidence

If you're lacking in any of them, you're not going to be able to charge as much. It's as simple as that.

Experience

When you're first starting out you lack the experience and you won't be able to charge a premium. Don't worry, you'll work your way up. But you need to understand that you're starting at the bottom, you're untested, you have no track record and the rate you can charge is going to reflect that.

Knowledge

The more you know, the more expertise you can provide, the more you can justifiably charge. This is good news, because if you're lacking in experience you can make up for it with knowledge. You can always learn more, grow and add to the value you offer clients.

Confidence

No matter how much experience or knowledge you have, if you lack confidence your rates are going to be low. You need to be able to stand up to clients, stick to your guns and insist on the rate you deserve. If you have the confidence to back it up, your clients will come around. If you're not so sure you have what it takes, your clients will sense your weakness and they'll want a cheaper price.

Story: Quoting Projects

BILL ERICKSON, FREELANCE DEVELOPER

What are some best practices that help you become a successful freelancer?

My business background was the biggest part of my success. A lot of developers don't have that and I would encourage them to go learn what they need. I see the feast or famine cycle way too often with developers. When they finish one project they turn around and have nothing to do next. They need to manage their pipeline, schedule effectively and learn to say no.

You need to know the type of projects that will mess up your schedule or won't be profitable. I say no to 80 percent of what people ask me to do. It's not always because I can't do the task. It's often because it wouldn't be profitable or would lead to a poor experience for the client based on their expectations.

Analytics is another tool I use. I built a customer relations management (CRM) system on top of WordPress to keep track of prospects, active projects and data.

Three to four years ago I was finally booked up and I was trying to decide which projects to take. It was a mixed bag. Sometimes I'd have really profitable projects, sometimes a project would drag on forever. How could I predict it? So I started collecting data. I used time tracking programs, entered the price I quoted, the hours I spent, etc. I could calculate the effective hourly rate, sort and see what the characteristics of a good project were.

What I learned is that the smaller the site, the more I was able to make on it. I could quote it more effectively and give more value in less time, which meant I could charge more.

So that pivoted my business. Now I'm pivoting toward larger projects.

You need to be making data-driven decisions, rather than going off your gut. Because often your gut is wrong.

What is it about smaller sites that you found more profitable?

There's an inherent value in a website to a business. So regardless of the time you put in to the job, there's value. At the smaller level, I'm doing more of the same things, so I can increase my efficiency. I can build it faster while delivering the same value. But the more custom it becomes, the more time you're devoting to this client that you can never reuse. So your value approaches the time you put in.

So the first three hours of a project might deliver $2,000 worth of value. But the more time I put in, you're getting maybe $200 of value for each hour. So as time increases, the value flattens. I can deliver a ton of value quickly. The more unique your needs, the less value you perceive and more time I have to put in.

But lately you've been doing larger sites?

That's where my business is now going. I priced myself out of the small end. There are too many developers offering the smaller sites. I can do that for past clients who have seen the difference, but many prospective clients can't tell the difference between an average developer and a good one.

For the past year or so I've been focusing on larger sites. For instance the University of Cambridge hired me to build a WordPress site that encompasses their new brand, and are rolling it out across 80 different domains.

It's a higher level of WordPress development, really testing the bounds of what can be done with WordPress. They needed a senior developer.

I'm currently collecting data on every aspect of the process to deliver better quotes. How much time did I spend on all these things? I document it so when it comes time to quote another project, I know how much I need to charge.

You'll have an innate feeling—I know this project will drag on, so I have to charge more. You want to turn innate feelings into data points you can do something with, turn it into usable data.

How do you handle scope creep, when clients keep asking for new stuff?

Scope creep is another reason why I tended toward smaller projects. By focusing on smaller projects with a more defined scope I could do better at limiting scope creep.

For larger projects with areas we know can't be defined, identify those areas and structure your quote appropriately. I'll use a fixed bid for the defined scope, and time-based billing for aspects we can't lock down initially.

I built a site for Reader's Digest recently. We had a clear scope for the most part, for which I provided a fixed bid. But they needed a bbPress forum to replace a custom forum they had built in-house.

My quote covered just the installation and styling of bbPress, it did not include any custom functionality, but stated that would be billed at my hourly rate. Once we reviewed the site with bbPress, we could identify what custom features they also wanted developed.

> It's important to identify areas that are clear and identify areas where you can't have a clear scope and change your quote accordingly.

Understand Value

As you're trying to sell your services you'll quickly learn that not all clients are equal. Some understand the value you can deliver—not merely the cost of the website, but the value that website is going to bring to their business.

Smart clients are willing to pay for that.

They understand the value you bring to their business will pay for itself over and over again. (That's how marketing works.) So they're willing to invest.

Other clients are—well, how do we put this nicely? They're cheap. They want to save money. They want the cheapest price. That's not to say you can't serve those clients, but they have a different understanding of value.

Some clients might have a good understanding of value, but they don't have the money to pay for it. These are clients who will seek out an expert and do whatever they can to get that expert insight. They would rather spend half their budget on brilliant insight and wisdom and then pay for a low budget site they know how to improve. Spending twice as much on a website might sound smarter, but a client is likely to get more value from that brilliant business insight.

So you need to understand value.

It's not simply a 'time for money' equation. Many hourly rate freelancers get stuck in that mindset and truly limit their earning potential. Because there are only so many hours in the day, so many days in the week, so many weeks in their year. And you want to have a life.

Here's another way to think about it: **There is a lot more that goes into the work you do than the exact amount of time it takes you to do the work.** It may only take you three hours to build out a simple website. But years of experience have gone into those three hours.

You've learned—the hard way—what not to do, how to avoid problems and make that site awesome.

Simply charging an hourly rate for those three hours might miss out on the years of value that went into doing that job in three hours instead of 13 hours.

The more you can understand the value you can deliver and the more you can help your clients see that value, the more you can charge.

Story: Selling Value

JAMES DALMAN, FREELANCE DESIGNER

As a teenager I had a business doing custom airbrushing and artwork. At the time I thought I was making good money: I was charging $20 per hour.

One day, my best friend's grandfather asked me for a bid on two custom murals. He wanted his name and logo painted on the side of his transmission shop. So I did what I always did—I followed a formula from an artist's guidebook and worked up my estimate.

I figured how many hours it would take and calculated the cost based on my hourly rate. I accounted for materials and expenses. Then I added a minuscule profit on top, just in case I needed an extra hour or two to complete the project.

Seemed reasonable.

Then I had to make the pitch. I started explaining my rates, justifying the time and cost. In the middle of it the old man stopped me:

"Son, I don't give a damn about your rates and your time."

It felt like a slap in the face.

"Just give me a price on the value you are delivering for me," he went on. "If you do the work in an hour or in 40 hours, I could care less. Just give me a quote."

And then I realized it wasn't a slap, it was the best business advice I would ever hear.

He continued to explain to me that business owners or customers don't want to hear about how many hours it takes to do a project. They don't care about your expenses or profits. **What they care about is value.** The value and benefits you deliver are really what people want.

He told me profitability would come through being efficient. If I could do the work faster without compromising quality, I'd make a lot more money. And if I sold on value, it didn't matter if the project was completed in an hour or 100 hours. What mattered was the final outcome.

Hourly vs. Per Project

Understanding value is important in figuring out what you can charge. There are two common approaches: Hourly rates and per project rates. They both have their benefits and you'll have to decide for yourself.

Pros & Cons of Hourly Rates:

- Ideal if you don't know how long the job will take.
- Protects you when clients ask for above and beyond the needs of the job, which they often do.
- Can make it easier to estimate your own financial needs.
- Boosts your perceived value ("They must be good if they charge X")
- But that high rate may also scare clients away.
- If you're slow the sticker shock will freak your client out.
- If you work fast you're robbing yourself of additional income.
- Clients might be turned off by the open-ended nature of an hourly rate and the potential cost.
- It's tempting to take your time and dishonestly milk the clock.

Pros & Cons of Per Project Rates:

- A flat rate makes everything clear to everyone involved and makes negotiation easier.
- You can easily outsource work and mark up the cost.
- You can make substantially more money if you work fast.
- You can also lose money a number of ways: working too slow, a project that gets out of hand or misjudging how long it will take.
- You have to spell out deliverables clearly and be able to draw the line with a client asking for more changes. This is absolutely critical.

In the end you'll need to decide what works best for you. One good approach is to do a little of both.

Give a flat, per project rate but then include an hourly rate for changes and revisions that go beyond the original agreement. Or use a per project rate for most work, but use an hourly rate for consulting, training or on-site work.

Or use an hourly rate but give your clients an estimated range for how long you think the project will take.

You might want to start off by quoting your hourly rate until you can better estimate how long it will take you to do a project. Then switch to per project rates.

Story: Billing

BILL ERICKSON, FREELANCE DEVELOPER

Can you tell us about your unique billing system?

For all my projects I require 25% down to get it on the calendar. When the project starts I invoice for the remaining 75%, due one week after the project is ready for review. So if it takes three weeks for initial development, payment is due in four weeks.

I tie it to the start so it's tied to a deliverable on my end. I've put in 90% of the work so far and you've seen it, so it's your turn to put trust in me. If you're waiting for the site to go live for final payment, it can take quite a while to get paid, and there's not much you can do to speed it up. I have sites on my server that have been there for a year as clients tweak content—I don't want an invoice tied up in that. It motivates them to get their work done.

On larger projects we'll break it down with larger milestones, so functionality is reviewed on certain dates.

> **But payment is always based on a deliverable on my schedule, rather than a client's deliverable such as approval.** You're aligning motivation. If they know that once it's approved they owe you $5,000, they're less motivated to approve it. If they've already paid for the site, they want it live as soon as possible and are more likely to accomplish their tasks.
>
> Once final payment comes in, then the site can be launched. Once the site is approved and migrated, they have 10 days to identify any migration-related issues. After 10 days, the project is complete and I remove it from my development server. Further changes are billed on a time basis.

Ask for Budgets

When you're talking to a client it can be hard to figure out exactly how much they're willing to spend. They might have a good understanding of value and they might not. They might have budget to spend and they might not. How much of that budget they're willing to spend might be an entirely different question.

Here are some tips on how to get a better handle on a client's budget so you can give a better quote:

1. Just Ask

Sometimes the simplest thing to do is just come right out and ask, "What's your budget?"

Some clients will answer right away. Others will stall or give some gibberish that really means they don't have a lot of money.

If you don't get a solid answer you can do two things. First, be silent. Let it be awkward for a minute.

Sometimes that will force a client to come out with it. Second, explain that you're asking to figure out if you're the best fit for them, and then give them some price ranges. Maybe under $2,000, $2,000 to $10,000 and something over that.

It quickly gets to the heart of the matter when you start talking about specific dollar amounts. You'll learn where a customer is at in terms of value and what they're able and willing to spend. And remember there is no wrong answer.

A client might start out with a small budget, but as you educate them about the value you can bring to a project, they're willing to spend more.

2. Anchor & Discount

In their book *Pricing Explained: How to Sell on Value & Earn More Per Project*, James Dalman and Chris Lema talk about the anchor and discount method. This approach emphasizes perceived value. The idea is to make a pitch starting with your full, ideal solution. That's the anchor. It's where negotiation starts. Then you offer discounts that lower the price but also significantly reduce the value.

So maybe you start with a web project that has all the extras—competitive analysis, custom logo creation, a design that leverages their brand, on-going site management and custom features to drive lead generation. You charge $10,000 for that approach.

But you acknowledge that not everyone can afford that, and offer to remove the logo design, the competitive analysis and the custom theme development for half the price ($5,000).

Then you offer an even more reduced approach with no on-going site management for $2,500.

You've just given a client a huge range for both price and value. It will be a lot easier to talk about budget and what they really need now that they see the range of options.

Set Your Terms

One important lesson for freelancers is to set your own rules. You don't have to play by whatever rules your client lays down. You should have your own rules and work to get the client to play by your rules as much as you can.

Like any business arrangement there may need to be some give and take involved. But setting your own terms is a big part of protecting yourself and also your client.

If you don't set your terms you risk getting screwed over by your client's terms, or worse, being left in the lurch when there's no agreement at all.

You want to get paid and your client wants their job done, ideally without bringing in any lawyers.

If things go south, you both want to be able to walk away without any hard feelings. The best way you can assure that outcome is by setting your own terms.

Standard Business Terms

There are all kinds of rules and terms you could stipulate, but here are some minimum terms you should include:

- **Payment terms:** How much are they paying, when are they paying, when is it due, what happens if it's late, how are they paying, etc. You want to spell out and agree on the details.

- **Project details:** What are you doing for the project? It's easy to keep this vague, but you want to be very specific about what work you're doing and what work you're not doing. This is important to avoiding scope creep. A good way to keep this in check is to stipulate how many revisions or changes you'll do.

- **Rates:** Even if you quoted a flat rate for your project, it can be helpful to include your rate for additional work above and beyond the project stipulations.

- **Refunds and cancelations:** What happens if the project goes south? Maybe your client isn't happy with your work. Or maybe you have an emergency and need to completely bail on the project. What happens? Do you get paid for work completed even if it's not delivered? Does your client get a full refund? These can be some of the most contentious issues, so spell some basics out ahead of time.

- **Methodology and communication:** This is a good place to detail anything about your working relationship that you want to control. If you only want to communicate via email (and avoid the time suck of phone calls), put it in your terms. If you are only available during certain hours, make that known. If you need certain approvals, responses and feedback from the client, put some parameters in the contract.

- **Self-promotion:** Include some fine print that you can use the project for self-promotion and add it to your portfolio.

- **Timeline:** Detail the project deadline, any milestones, and what happens if deadlines are missed on either side. Make it clear that a delay on their end equals a delay on your end, pushing your deadline back (this is a big one!).

- **Expiration date:** For quotes or proposals be sure to include an expiration date. This creates a sense of urgency and allows you to raise your price if a client comes back months later and your situation has changed. Maybe you get super busy and don't want to honor a lower price you quoted when your schedule was bare.

- **Delivery of assets:** Spell out how the final project is delivered.

Contract

Once you decide on those terms, you should write them into a contract. You might even want to have a lawyer look over your terms and make sure everything works.

Some people are loathe to involve the lawyers, and that's fine, but it's still important to put your terms in writing and get agreement from your client. Maybe you work up a 'service agreement' document that you have your clients sign. This might sound more formal than your happy handshake agreement way of doing business, but it's an important part of protecting yourself.

Get Paid Up Front

A good practice to protect yourself is to insist on half the payment up front before you start any work and the rest of the payment when the job is finished.

If it's a long term project involving a lot of money, you may want to set up a payment schedule that compensates you for the work as you go along. And make sure you get that final payment before you hand over all the finished work.

What Do You Expect

You can think of all of this as expectation management. It's a good way to keep a happy client relationship.

What does your client think the project is going to entail?

What do you think the project is going to entail?

Often those two perspectives don't match up. The more you can bring them in line and get everybody on the same page, the more you'll avoid sudden surprises. Those surprises can quickly sour a relationship and lead to an ugly project that nobody wants to repeat.

When in doubt, list it out.

- **Client responsibilities:** Don't forget that all these expectations aren't just on your end. You have expectations of your client and those should be detailed in your terms.

- **Scope creep:** If you've done the work of including all your terms in your contract, you should avoid scope creep. Remember that it's your responsibility to tell your client when a request goes outside the scope of the project and either don't do it or charge them accordingly.

- **It's OK to say no:** Stick to your guns. Sometimes you'll have to say no and walk away. But if a client won't agree to reasonable terms then you probably wouldn't want to work with them anyway.

Nobody is going to look out for you as a freelancer, so you need to stand up for yourself and care enough to set your terms and stick to them.

Story: Contracts

BILL ERICKSON, FREELANCE DEVELOPER

How do you handle contracts?

I'm a little different than most developers because I don't use super legalese contracts no one understands. I see the purpose of a contract as setting expectations—it says what I do and what you do. This is a document we refer to throughout our project.

If I send a site in for review and they say something isn't there, we go back to the contract to see what it says. If you make the contract overly complicated, the client won't read it and there could be misunderstandings. My contract is an email, it explains the scope of the work, gives payment terms, timelines, and other topics that I find important to have in writing.

I've had a few clients not pay me and I could have sued them, but it's not worth it for a $2,000 project. I can sacrifice a little legal security with the few clients who won't pay in exchange for better understanding and communication on my other projects. I'm definitely in the minority on that end. I know high-end developers all have really big legal contacts.

Does that approach to contracts work for the bigger projects?

For my larger projects, the clients typically have a contractor's agreement I have to sign anyway, so this is more of a functional document, the one we refer to throughout the project. I go through their contract and make sure it matches the terms of mine.

They often want to own copyrights to everything, so I include a GPL statement:

"WordPress is an open-source project. The code we use to run your site has been freely developed by thousands of developers. If I develop any useful piece of code that can be generalized and used to further the WordPress project, I will contribute it as a tutorial, plugin, or patch to WordPress core. However, I will never resell or give away the code to your website in whole to another party."

Most clients don't have a problem with it once you phrase it like that, and it's important to agree to this before you start developing. Lawyers don't like it though. I once had a contact that said I couldn't use GPL software—it was a WordPress site so we had to update their contract.

I've never had a client have an issue with that. When I say I'll never give away the full site or code to a competitor, they're happy. They hired me because they saw what I've done through my contributions to the WordPress community. That's part of their purchasing decision. If they hired me because of all this stuff, they won't ask me to stop.

Let's Make a Deal

This can be uncomfortable for some people, but you need to be willing to negotiate each project. Here are a few quick negotiating tips:

- Be confident in your skills and talent. Don't let anyone belittle you or make you think you're charging too much.
- Sell the benefits of your services, not the service itself. Don't focus on the website you're going to build, focus on what the website will do for them. How does it save them time, money, frustration? How does it improve their reputation, the bottom line, etc? That's worth paying for.
- Take the time to educate your clients about what you're offering and why it's valuable.

They'll be more willing to pay when they realize what SEO is and how it helps them. Emphasize value.

- Be a good listener. Sometimes a client may have an objection, but they're not coming out and saying what it is. By listening you can often figure it out.
- Have some mutual give and take. If a client balks at your rate, offer a lower rate but also offer fewer revisions and a later deadline.
- Don't fall for cheap excuses. Don't take a smaller rate now on the promise of future work.
- It's OK to say no. If you're not comfortable or something doesn't feel right, walk away. It's better to be safe than sorry. Trust your instincts.

Story: Hiring People

JUSTIN SAINTON, FREELANCE DEVELOPER, ZAO

You brought on your first employee in 2014. How did you know you were ready?

I hired my first person in 2009, and I made the mistake of hiring for sales. I thought that was a great call—let me focus on what I like, and someone else could handle sales. But it never worked out. The mistake I made was to hire sales out, instead of doing it myself as the person who knows what we're selling and what we can do.

So now, fast forward five years, and we've hired Liz. She's amazing. She doesn't do sales—she does development, on-boarding and admin. The reason I think it's worked well this time around is that it still lets me focus on what I like to do. Now we're in a place where sales come in at a much higher volume and quality.

Five years ago I felt like we really needed someone pounding the pavement and bringing leads in. Now we have the experience to know what we actually need.

How did going from a solo shop to having employees change things?

You spend more time teaching and managing. When you go from one to two, you're essentially cutting back the work you do by 25% and spending a good quarter of your time mentoring, teaching and training.

I have no ambition to grow to a 20- or 30- or 40-person company, I've always been very happy with the idea of a small team, like 5 to 8 people. That's the vision we have. At the rate we're going that may take 60 years.

It changes some things for sure. I have to be more intentional about my time. I have less ability to just have my head stuck in the code than I used to. You have someone else you're responsible for both financially and making sure they're having a happy work experience. You have to communicate early and often, really over-communicate. It's a learning process.

Systems & Processes

If you want to be successful as a freelancer you need to be efficient. You can't be losing things or reinventing the wheel every time you do something. You need a system to take care of stuff, a process for everything you do.

Benefits of a system:

- Consistent results for your clients.
- Keep yourself and your clients accountable.
- Stop items from slipping through the cracks.

- More efficiency equals more profitability.
- Train team members to take over quickly so you can walk away.

You want to create a process for every part of your business. Anything you do repeatedly is something you can systemize, and that's how you get more efficient.

It's not overkill. These kinds of checklists and processes will make you a successful freelancer.

Here are some different steps in your process that could use a system:

Potential Client Contact

However you handle that first contact with a potential client, whether it's a phone call, email or handshake, make sure you respond promptly, gather as many details as possible and pre-qualify the prospect.

Examples:
For email or web forms have a system to respond within one day and give your potential client two options to move forward: 1. Fill out an online questionnaire or assessment. 2. Set up a time for a call.

For contact by phone or in person, give them 15 minutes immediately if you're available. Direct them to your online questionnaire or schedule a longer consultation.

Sales

Selling yourself can be tough for a lot of freelancers. But if you want to succeed, you've got to get over the hesitation and figure out how to sell your services with confidence. Creating a sales system can be a good way to make the whole process easier.

Examples:

Use an assessment or questionnaire that potential clients fill out online to get an idea of what they need. Follow up with a phone call or email to clarify anything and answer any outstanding questions. This should focus on what they need and how you can deliver value. Put together a proposal that you cut and paste from existing templates. Don't reinvent the wheel every time you do this. Finally, you should end your sales process with an invoice to get the first payment and kick off the project. Don't start work until you've got money in the bank.

Discovery

Sometimes the sales phase isn't enough and you need to know more about your client. This is where you'll have to figure out your exact process. For some people the discovery phase happens alongside sales. For others it's something that happens once you have a contract in place and you're getting paid for it.

This is usually working with the client to figure out what they need. You're doing consulting and helping them sort through what they have, what they need and how it all fits together. You might not know exactly what a client needs yet, so you're doing this work to help them figure it out and then give them an actual quote for the project. Just make sure you're getting paid for this work.

You could charge separately for this service or you could work into a standard package that includes discovery and maybe has some flexibility depending on the results of your work.

This is another great place to create a process and systems. You should have standard templates and forms to help a client work through questions and issues.

Design

This is where the magic happens. But you still need a system. Even though it's creative work, you can be even more creative within the confines of a system.

Having a process will ensure you don't miss anything, allow you to track time and improve your efficiency (and profitability), and you're creating a system you can train others to do (staff members, interns, students).

Example design process:

- Wireframes
- Feedback and approval of wireframes
- Design comps created
- Feedback and revisions (if necessary)
- Design approval
- Double check and finalize all files
- Upload files, fonts and support materials (assuming someone else is doing the development)

Development

You should also create a system for how you go about setting up a site. Just like the design, you want to work systematically through the process. This way you can create shortcuts to improve your process.

One typical shortcut is to create a sandbox WordPress installation that has a bare theme framework you can start from, as well as all the plugins you install for your clients. You can use a tool such as BackupBuddy to duplicate this installation on your development server.

Be sure your development process includes a review with the client, a limit on changes, and a system for launching the site.

Launch

Once the site is launched, you want to check again for any final tweaks and make sure everything is working the way it's supposed to. Deliver the appropriate logins to the client and do any training you've included in your proposal. If you're doing on-going maintenance, you'll want to move the project over to whatever process you have for that. If your client is running things, you'll want to pass everything off and wipe your hands of it. But then have a process in places to check back with them (more on that later).

Once the site is live, you should add it to your portfolio and brag about it on social media.

Touch base with your client and congratulate them on a finished project. Let them know you're available if they need anything else and ask for a testimony or any feedback on improving their experience. A glowing review is a good thing to add to your portfolio.

Post Launch

One of the best things you can do as a freelancer is to stay in touch with your clients after you finish their project.

It's a great way to show you care about the client and it builds brand equity. Plus, you can get additional work by following up.

Make a plan to follow up. Put it on your calendar to give them a call or an email in three months (and yes, have a template for that email).

Services

So you're a freelance web designer. You might think your list of services is pretty basic—you build websites.

But it shouldn't be that simple.

There are a lot of other services you can offer as a freelancer that go beyond simply building websites. You can sell maintenance, security and training services. You can also create stuff, whether it's themes and plugins or writing books. Many of these services can be turned into recurring revenue where you're able to continuously charge clients.

You want to offer a broader slate of services because it gives clients some options. They might not even realize they need help with security, but if you package it up and offer it as a service, that's more money in your pocket.

In many cases you might be offering these things anyway. But by pulling them out as separate services you can often charge more. You're highlighting the value of the service and helping clients see why they should pay for it.

Recurring Revenue

One of the big challenges of freelancing is the ebb and flow of client work. It's a relentless feast or famine cycle. But selling recurring revenue packages can be one way to break out of that cycle and increase your business.

You can develop recurring revenue a lot of different ways, but we want to focus on packaged services where a client pays you a monthly fee for a particular set of tasks. Usually it's a clearly defined package where you can deliver ongoing value and your clients get stuff done that they don't have the time or skill to do themselves. In the ideal recurring revenue situation you're delivering lots of value with minimal effort. It's steady work for you and your client gets some needed expertise. Win, win.

Here's what you want from a recurring revenue situation:

Consistent, dependable monthly income doing good work for great clients.

- *"Consistent dependable monthly income"* – This will stabilize your workload, giving you a foundation to build on.

- *"Doing good work"* – It might not be your all-time favorite work, but it's going to be good stuff you can do well and you enjoy.

- *"For great clients"* – You're looking for clients who trust you and will pay you well to do what you do best. They understand they don't have the time or expertise to do it themselves, but you do.

Recurring Revenue Benefits for Freelancers

Setting up recurring work with a client is a huge win for you as a freelancer. It can take a lot of the stress out of freelancing and give you stability. Let's look at the benefits:

Consistent Revenue

The feast or famine cycle is one of the constant challenges for freelance work.

One month you're swamped: feast. You've got so much work coming in that you're working late into the night to keep up with it. **But then the next month you've got nothing: famine.** You're twiddling your thumbs and checking Facebook all day.

It's a continual cycle that builds on itself, because every time you go through a famine period, you're so desperate for work you say yes to everything, which builds into another time of feast. It's a good way to burn yourself out, never mind go out of business.

But when you put clients on a recurring revenue package you build stability and consistency into your business. Suddenly you have a better idea what you're going to make next month and you can plan on it. You can say no to projects that don't fit because you have something to fall back on. You can more confidently pursue projects you want because you have a stable base of recurring revenue to rely on.

Work With the Best Clients

Another big benefit of recurring revenue for freelancers is that you can work with the best clients. Because you have consistent work—a safety net—you have more freedom to pick and choose your clients. You're not saying yes to every project that comes in the door just because you're terrified of facing another famine cycle.

You can also work with your best clients consistently. Find your favorite client to work with and sign them up on a recurring revenue package. **If people are a joy to work with, work with them more.** Offer them a little discount for some consistency, and then enjoy working with better clients.

Plus, clients who are willing to do a recurring revenue arrangement understand the value of your work. These aren't going to be disgruntled clients who keep dismissing your efforts or input. These are the keepers.

Build Your Business

The feast or famine cycle is kind of like the classic fight or flight response. Something happens and you react—without thinking, without planning, without considering the options. You just react. It's not a great way to run a business.

You want your business to be responsive and react to changing markets—but not like a cornered animal. You should have a plan. You should have some direction. You should have control over where your business is going.

Generating recurring revenue can give you the freedom to build your business. The stability of recurring revenue gives you the time and resources to think, to plan, to consider options. **You can build your business the way you want instead of just reacting to whatever is happening.**

It's a Lot of Work to Get a Client

You put a lot of effort into scoring a new client. Why would you want to do a single project with them and then not see them again for a long time? That's the downside of web development. You build someone a site and they're set for a few years. They're not likely to need a new site a few months down the road.

So don't waste your efforts bringing in clients by only doing one project with them. Do that initial project to build trust and show how much value you can offer. Then pitch them a recurring revenue package and secure their business for the future.

Recurring Revenue Benefits for Clients

OK, so recurring revenue sounds like a pretty great deal for you as a freelancer. But what about your clients? How is this better for them?

It's an important question to answer because you have to turn around and sell this deal to your clients. So it has to be a win-win. And it is.

Like any business, your clients want to do their work well. They want to grow their business, build their brand, sell their stuff and be on the cutting edge doing it. But like any business, they face struggles. That's where you can help.

You can come in as a consistent partner who can help them overcome their struggles. They can have all kinds of struggles:

- Maybe they don't know what to do and you can help them sort it out as a consultant.
- Maybe they know the what, but they don't know the how. Your job is to come in and make it happen.
- Maybe they lack the time, energy or focus to do these things. That's where you can pick up the slack for them.
- It could be an issue where their time is better spent on their expertise. Most good business people will recognize their own weaknesses and hire someone who's good at what they're not. You can be the one who excels where they don't.
- Your clients also might just have too many balls in the air and they need someone to help them keep up. You're taking on the extra workload so nothing gets dropped.

You can come in and help a client get done what they need to get done. That's a huge help.

But why do it on a recurring basis?

Help Your Clients Be Consistent

Doing it consistently on a recurring revenue model means that it's continually getting done. It's not something you come in and clean up every few months, only to turn around and find things in disarray again.

You want to help your client overcome their struggles for good, not just once in a while. And that's going to mean some consistent work.

Give Your Clients a Discount

That recurring revenue is a great help to you as a freelancer. So you should give your clients a corresponding discount. It's a win for you, so make it a win for them. That can be a major selling point for a client—they get more work out of you just by doing it consistently.

It's Sustainable For Them Too

A recurring revenue package helps stabilize your income, but it also helps stabilize your clients' expenses. When clients play catch up they're racking up the expenses and probably throwing the budget out of whack. But with your recurring revenue plan they can spread out the cost of doing all that work.

It's easier for your clients to plan and budget your recurring revenue fee than be surprised by a big catch-up project. Plus, cleaning up the disarray is going to be more expensive than simply keeping it maintained consistently.

Never Fear

Another good reason to help a client on a recurring revenue basis is that they never have to worry about it. If they're calling you up every time they run into a problem, and you're doing a separate estimate and invoice, it's just a lot of unnecessary work. They're spending more time than they need to worrying about it.

If they just hire you on a recurring revenue basis, you can deal with the whole thing and completely take it off their plate.

They don't have to keep track of it.

They don't have to follow up.

They don't have to wonder if they need to call in the freelancer again.

They can sit back and know it's taken care of. That's a good feeling for a busy entrepreneur.

Ongoing Help

Not only do clients not need to worry about it, but they know you're on top of it. Over time things will change and it's one more area they don't have to worry about keeping up. That's your job.

It's one thing to outsource the stuff you can't do and feel good knowing it's being done right. It's another thing to have that work done consistently, so you know it's not just done right once, but repeatedly.

It's the difference between calling the police and having your own security.

It's the difference between taking your car to a mechanic when it breaks and having a mechanic on hand to keep your car running in the first place.

Don't wait for something to break to fix it. By keeping you on a recurring revenue basis, your clients can have things properly tuned and working well, rather than waiting for the wheels to fall off. **Maintenance is a lot cheaper than catastrophic repairs.**

Marketing Recurring Revenue

As you think about what your clients need, focus on the outcomes and results they want to see, as well as the hassles, struggles and obstacles they face in achieving those results.

You can be the solution.

Explore some of those issues and make sure you're working them into your marketing materials. Constantly emphasize how you're saving them hassle and delivering real outcomes. You want to give your clients good value.

What outcomes/results do they want?
- Consistent help from a dependable, knowledgeable partner
- Look good, hip, cutting edge
- Sell stuff online
- Expand business
- Increase brand exposure
- Build community

What hassles, struggles and obstacles do they have doing it?

- Knowing what to do
- Knowing how to do it
- Not having time
- Not having energy
- Not having focus
- Need to use time better on their expertise
- Keeping up with everything

Recurring Revenue Services to Offer

There are a lot of different recurring revenue services you can offer, including marketing, maintenance, security, training and more.

We'll talk more specifically about some of those, but it's helpful to think through different ways you can package those services:

- **Strategy & Planning:** You're the expert guide who tells them what to do and they do the work.

- **Execution:** You handle the actual work and do it for them.

- **Training:** You train your client (or others) to do the work.

- **Emergency**: Be the 911 webmaster, ready to help in a pinch for a big premium.

Determine Your Services

Now it's time for you to sit down and list the recurring revenue services that would work for you. Get very specific about exactly what you're offering. Don't just do marketing, offer email newsletters or social media. Which areas sound appealing? Which ones sound horrible? — just cross them off the list. Look at the kind of work you like to do and think about what your clients continually ask for.

Put together a list of potential recurring revenue services. Be sure you're including lots of value.

Package & Price Your Services

Once you have a full list, start creating recurring revenue packages. Put things together in a way that would be appealing to your clients. Think about pricing and what's going to work for both you and your client. Remember to include a discount as you put your pricing together.

Create Your Marketing

Finally, you need to think through how you're going to sell your recurring revenue services. You'll want a sales page on your site, a list of benefits you can talk through with customers, a way to up-sell your current clients, etc.

Recurring Revenue Tips

Let's get practical. Here are some tips to help you put together your recurring revenue offerings:

- **Don't nickel and dime yourself:** Make sure you're offering real value, but don't keep adding in services to the point that you're spending hours and hours each month with these recurring services. You don't want to offer every client an hour per week and suddenly you're maxing out your allotted time each week.

- **Three packages:** When you put together packages, three is the magic number. Highlight one of them as the best deal and steer your clients in that direction.

- **Test with the best:** You want to refine your recurring revenue, so put together a plan and then test it with your best clients.

- **Always get better:** Recurring revenue is not a 'set it and forget it' business. You need to constantly refine your services, improving what you're offering and delivering for your clients. Otherwise that revenue won't keep recurring.

- **Show your skills:** Put on a webinar or write an ebook to demonstrate your expertise. Rather than giving away your secrets, this is showing your skills. Instead of poaching the best practices, smart clients will see you know your stuff and hire you to do it for them.

- **Maintain contact:** There's a temptation for maintenance services to be invisible for the client—after all, the whole point is that they shouldn't have to worry about it. But you want to maintain contact with them and show ongoing value. Your recurring revenue is their recurring expense, so make sure they also see recurring value.

Selling Maintenance

As a freelance developer you know WordPress needs to be kept up to date and too often clients don't bother. Then you get panicked calls about hacked sites.

Or some kind of oops makes a site disappear. They want you to bring it back right now, but they never paid you to set up any kind of backup system.

Or themes and plugins need to be updated but that simple click breaks something and a client needs immediate help.

You should offer a monthly WordPress maintenance package to your clients. You take care of the details and your client doesn't sweat it. To you they're relatively minor issues, often automated and simple; but to your clients they're business-stopping nightmares.

Who Needs WordPress Maintenance?

Who doesn't need it?

Current Clients

Most of your clients would probably love the opportunity to let someone else worry about all these technical details. It's something you can offer to current clients to continue the relationship and offer them extra service.

Former Clients

A good freelance business needs repeat customers, so go back to your past clients and try selling WordPress maintenance packages to them. Be the hero as you point out problems and then take care of them.

New Clients

It's also something you can offer to entice new clients. There are plenty of small and mid-level organizations with no internal web team. They've got websites they outsource and details like security and backups are a constant worry.

Nonprofits are another area where you'll likely find organizations without any developers on staff. Many nonprofits are creating amazing content online, but they're often handcuffed by a lack of technical help. They need to keep that content safe and want to make some tweaks, but bringing in a developer sounds pricey. They probably have no idea how affordable ongoing WordPress maintenance could be.

What to Include in Your WordPress Maintenance Package?

You can bundle all kinds of services when you're selling WordPress maintenance. Put together a package that works. It all depends on what you're comfortable with and what you think your clients need. Here are some potential services you could include:

- **Updates:** WordPress usually rolls out major updates twice a year, though minor updates roll out as needed. There are also updates for themes and plugins, which are much less predictable.

- **Backups:** Sites should have a backup plan that fits with their needs. A site with lots of content updates might want a database backup once a day at a minimum and a full backup weekly.

Sites with fewer updates might not need such frequent backups, but they should still have regularly scheduled, full-site backups that are stored off-site.

- **Tracking & Reporting:** Pulling up stats isn't very difficult, but it's the kind of thing a lot of website owners don't have time for and can't always make sense of. Offering a simple report that summarizes numbers and includes a few trends or other basics (sales numbers, increases in email or social media subscribers) could be very helpful.

- **Hosting & Domain Name:** Especially for new clients you can offer the whole package and include their domain registration and hosting as well. Many hosts offer reseller accounts and rolling this into a site's maintenance and updates means you've got the entire site covered.

- **Other Services:** You might sweeten your retainer by adding specific services offered in limited hourly chunks. For example, you might offer 10 hours of tech tweaks per month. It could be coding, design, writing, SEO improvements or even training or support.

What's the Cost?

Once you figure out what you're going to offer for ongoing WordPress maintenance, then you need to sort out how much to charge.
This will depend on your expenses, so be sure to add up all your costs:

- **Plugins:** You'll want some plugins to help with monitoring and maintenance.

- **Tools:** If you're managing a lot of sites you'll want to make it easy on yourself. iThemes Sync will let you manage updates for multiple WordPress sites in one simple dashboard.

- **Storage:** Off-site backup is a must and it's easy with BackupBuddy. But you'll need storage space. BackupBuddy Stash offers free space with BackupBuddy, or you could also look into other options including Amazon S3 or Dropbox.

- **Hosting:** Look at your reseller hosting account to figure out what hosting and domains will cost and what you can charge.

- **Time:** Don't forget to factor in your time. While a lot of these maintenance tasks are easy and some are even automated, you still have some work to do and it's going to take some time. At the very least you need to set things up and keep an eye on them.

Make sure you're looking at the costs for all the services you include in your package. It should be a good deal for your clients because you're taking care of their needs and the steady work should entitle them to a discount. But be careful not to sell yourself short. You're providing a hugely valuable service and taking a major headache off your clients' plates.

Tip: Create a Workflow

As you think about how much time you're going to invest for each site, you should list out each required step and put together a workflow. Find ways to minimize time and maximize your efficiency.

Story: Dave Clements

DAVE CLEMENTS, FREELANCE DEVELOPER, THE WP BUTLER

What pushed you to get into selling WordPress maintenance plans?

When I would have clients ask me to do a task on their site after having built their site months or years before, I would undoubtedly be horrified to see numerous updates waiting to be done. In addition, the clients didn't have regular backups of their site, so I saw an opportunity to capitalize on an existing relationship, with trust already built, to recommend and carry out these maintenance tasks on the clients' behalf.

How has it worked for you? What benefits are you seeing for your business?

It's been a nice little vertical for my web development business. Once I complete someone's site, I can educate them on the need to maintain their site properly, and offer the service. To sweeten the deal, as an existing client, I also offer them a coupon code. It has the really nice benefit of allowing me to continue the relationship beyond just the development phase, so whenever they have a new need for their site, I'm always the first person on their mind.

What's changed since you started selling WordPress maintenance?

Not much has changed in my approach. The biggest change I've made is the cost of my development time. I really undervalued it to begin with and it was a big mistake.

> Once just a few clients have access to one or two hours of development time each and they aren't paying much for it, you're quickly losing money. So I modified that to more accurately reflect my cost and my expertise, and those who share those values are happy to pay for it, so we're all happy.

Selling Security

With major security breaches and hacker strikes, there's a lot to worry about on the web today. Your freelance clients are concerned, rightly so, and that's an opportunity for you to step in and help. **Selling WordPress security monitoring can make you the hero.**

By branching out and adding this to your freelance services, you're creating a new and steady income stream for yourself while also easing the fears of your clients. Selling WordPress security monitoring is a win, win.

What Does Selling WordPress Security Mean?

So what are you actually going to sell your clients? That's a good question and it's really up to you, but we can offer some suggestions:

1. Protection

First and foremost, you need to protect your clients' sites. You need to roll out some security measures to stop the hackers, prevent the breaches and keep them safe.

This will involve standard upfront work to put all your security measures in place. You might want to charge for this separately or require a long-term contract to cover your initial expenses.

2. Detection

Next you need to keep an eye on the perimeter and monitor what kind of shenanigans are going down on your clients' sites. You need to know when attacks are happening, know when things are getting bad and if there might be potential vulnerabilities you can plug up.

This should be an ongoing service that allows you to charge a monthly or annual fee.

3. Recovery

You need to be prepared to help your clients get back on their feet. No matter how good your security is, things happen. You need to be upfront with your client about this—no security is 100%. But you can help clean up. You can offer recovery and restoration services, from fixing hacks to completely restoring sites from a backup.

Some of this work will be part of your initial setup—creating backup systems for example—but you also might need to line up the big guns to call in if things get really ugly.

4. Education

For all the security measures you put in place for your client, you're not the only one in charge of their security. A lot of security comes down to what they do. If they have a horrible password or give admin level access to their entire company, your security efforts will be compromised.

You might want to create a PDF to cover some basic advice about passwords and best security practices. This is a good way to educate and protect your clients, while also reducing your liability.

Package It Up

You'll want to figure out what selling WordPress security looks like for you. Create a list of services you can offer and put together some packages.

Be Clear What You Offer

However you package your WordPress security monitoring, you need to make it clear what you're offering and what you're not. Your clients need to understand that there's always a risk—selling WordPress security is about minimizing risk and allowing for quick recovery. You can't promise perfect protection.

You should also make it clear what happens if your security measures fail and your clients' site is hacked. You might need to bring in a security contractor to clean things up. Who pays for that? Is it part of your package or is it an additional charge? Make sure it's clear upfront. You should either be charging more to cover the dreaded 'what if?' or your client should know the potential for additional costs.

Count the Cost

Be sure you're considering all the costs of selling WordPress security monitoring. You're going to have some initial fixed costs—plugins, time, set up—and some ongoing expenses as well.

You'll also have some potential costs that may or may not come into play. You never know what's going to happen. There could be a major attack and you'll be busy making sure everything is safe and reassuring your clients. You could have a breach and need to bring in a security contractor. Or maybe nothing will happen and you don't have any extra expenses.

But you don't know how it's going to work out and that's what your clients are paying for. They're paying not to worry about it, which means you have to.

When you set your prices you'll need to take all these things into account.

How to Sell WordPress Security Services

In some ways selling WordPress security services is easy. It sells itself. Just wait for another Internet security breach and watch your clients squirm with worry. Then you can resolve those fears by protecting their sites.

This can feel a bit predatory, and you really don't want to be the vulture freelancer who swoops in on distressed victims. But it is a reality that people are more open to their own security needs in the middle of a breach. It makes the threat real for everyone and they're motivated to act. Instead of preying on them, offer helpful advice and solutions. If you're working with previous clients you already have established trust to build on, so you're not an opportunist. Instead you're providing a valuable and wanted follow-up service.

Here are a few tips for how you can market your services:

- Make it part of a larger WordPress maintenance package and take care of all their ongoing tech needs. You'll be solving a major need and allowing them to focus on what they do best.

- Point out the increase in attacks on WordPress and how much hacker activity is really out there. Show them the actual number of attacks and attempts on their site. Those numbers can be scary.

But remember that your goal isn't to scare people, your goal is to take care of it for them. Show them a problem exists and help them solve it.

- Help them calculate how much their site is worth and what they'd lose if their site went down to hackers.

- Compare online security to real world security as a simple cost of doing business. Clients put locks on their doors and install security systems to protect their income—they should do the same online.

- Selling WordPress security services can be a part of every web development project you do. When you bid on a site, also include a pitch for the ongoing security monitoring to protect what they just paid you to build.

Get Started Selling WordPress Security

It's time to roll up your sleeves and get to work. What do you need to do to start selling WordPress security? Here's a checklist to get you started:

- Figure out exactly what you're going to offer and what kind of pricing structure you're going to have. You could even offer multiple levels of service (three levels with one highlighted as the best option is usually a good way to go).

- Get the tools you need. You'll need to buy some plugins, such as iThemes Security Pro, and familiarize yourself with how they work.

- Line up the extra services you'll need, whether it's off-site storage for backup or a security contractor to have on call (such as WP Security Lock or UnHack.Us).

- Put together an educational piece to share basic security practices with your client—especially stuff you don't have control over. This might be a PDF handout or you could create a series of short videos to walk clients through the basics of WordPress security.

- Create a page on your site for selling WordPress security monitoring.

- Add a pitch for security monitoring to your bid process.

- Develop a campaign to reach out to your previous clients to offer them security monitoring.

- Start beta testing. Find a couple clients and offer them a free trial or a reduced price beta test. Get everything set up and work out any kinks in your system.

Win, Win: Selling WordPress security is big win for both you and your clients. You get consistent, recurring income and your clients get the peace of mind that comes with solid security.

Story: Dan King

DAN KING, FREELANCE DEVELOPER, FISTBUMP MEDIA

What pushed you to get into selling WordPress maintenance plans?

As I was launching Fistbump Media, I wanted to be a resource for bloggers (and other brands) using my experience both as a writer and a technical expert. I knew that most bloggers get into blogging because they love to write, not because they want to be a webmaster.

So offering a service where I would essentially become the webmaster for them would take that stress off their plate and just allow them to focus on the piece they're really passionate about.

How has it worked for you? What benefits are you seeing for your business?

It's been great for me from a business standpoint! I charge $19.99 per month for a basic "managed hosting" plan. And I sometimes end up putting in a bit more work on some accounts than what I really budget. But when my sites are all running smoothly due to the routine maintenance, then most of them require very little extra personal attention. So it all kind of averages out. But as I'm building up a nice list of clients, it's quickly becoming a nice solid income stream for my growing business.

What's changed since you started offering ongoing maintenance?

Only my mindset for how I approach this piece of my business. I feel like I need to continually rethink how I do what I do.

For example, I'm starting to send my managed hosting clients a regular newsletter with tips, tricks and general advice based on what I'm seeing trending across their sites (things like spam management, etc.).

This kind of communication wasn't in my original plan, but then I found that many of my clients paid more and heard from me less often because things were running so smooth. And the lack of interaction could lead them to believe they're paying more for nothing. So dropping a line to everyone with some additional value-added stuff just lets them know that I'm working and looking out for their best interest.

> **What have you found to be the most effective way to sell ongoing maintenance?**
>
> Simply by selling the benefits! I just let people know that I manage the technology so that they can focus on doing what they do best.
>
> I also try to leverage trends… like a recent outage by a major hosting provider turned into several new clients for me simply due to the fact that I would actively manage security as part of the maintenance.
>
> The bottom line is that people don't want to have to worry about the technology, and that's what I try to tap into. Give them the freedom to be awesome, because they have a partner who just takes care of it for them.

Selling Training

Having a website is one thing, but knowing how to use it is another. And loving to use it, that's amazing.

You want your clients blogging with the best of them, adding images with ease and basically bragging about their site. To make that happen, you need to go the extra mile.

Simply coding a site isn't good enough. Any freelance developer can code a site and customizing the backend will help. But you want to go further and make sure your clients succeed. You need to train them—and train them well.

If you do it right—no second rate efforts allowed—your clients won't just find themselves with a web presence, they'll find success online. And your clients' success is ultimately your success.

Training as a Service

Offering training is a great way to make sure your clients get the most out of your services. But be sure to offer training as an actual service you're charging for. Either itemize it in your bids so the client can see the cost and the value or sell it separately. Another option is to roll it into your ongoing maintenance plan. Make yourself available for questions anytime and get a recurring payment for it. Clients get the security blanket of knowing you're always there and you get recurring income.

What WordPress Client Training Looks Like

Simply put, you need to school your client. Give 'em some education. You need to teach your client how to use WordPress, train them in the best practices and empower them to be successful.

Anything else is setting them up for failure—and their failure becomes your failure when they don't come back again and refuse to recommend you.

Training can happen in several different ways, but the important thing is that you offer something. Go above and beyond. Help your client make the most of their site, and everybody wins.

Pitfalls of WordPress Client Training

OK, so teaching your client how to use WordPress is a good idea. Everybody can agree on that.

But then we have some problems:
- You're not a teacher, you're a developer.
- You don't have the time to walk your client through the basics.
- WordPress changes all the time. How do you keep up with it?
- Where is it again? Clients easily lose and misplace things.
- There's a difference between knowing how and doing it well.

Ideally, your WordPress client training can address or avoid all of these pitfalls and help you get back to work faster while still keeping your clients happy.

How to Overcome the Training Hurdles

Here are a few ways to overcome those pitfalls and make your training efficient and effective:

1. Outsource

You're a techie, not a teacher. You might not be a people person. Maybe you don't do well in front of groups, or maybe you just don't have the time to learn webinar software. So it might make sense to outsource your training. Let a pro do it and tap into the many pre-existing resources created by people who are better teachers than you.

The only downside to outsourcing your training is that you'll likely be creating custom components for a client that won't be covered in someone else's generic training.

So even if you do outsource the basics, you might need to teach the custom bits yourself.

2. Create it Once

Every time you train a client, you're going to say the same thing. So don't reinvent the wheel. Create a generic resource you can share with multiple clients. Create it once and use it over and over again.

It's going to be some work to create this resource in the first place. You might be tempted to just schedule a training call and get it over with. But client after client after client—those calls are going to add up, and you'll waste your time. So create a training resource once and get back to work.

3. Make It Updatable

One of the biggest frustrations with creating training materials is that WordPress keeps changing. With every update those training materials become more out of date, so you're going to have to put some thought into keeping things current.

As you create your training materials, you need to do it in a way you can easily update. A PDF you hand off is going to get dated, so you might want to keep a version on your site that you keep current and give clients on-going access to. Or maybe you create a training site you host and update periodically, so clients can always get the latest and greatest.

This is another reason why outsourcing might be a good idea. Pay someone else to keep it current.

4. Make It Accessible

How many times have you sent a client a link, and they ask you to send it again? The reality is you aren't your client's highest priority, and the details about their website might get filed away and lost.

You can help by making your training materials easily accessible. Build them into the backend so they're always there. Add a help section to the menu so those resources are at their fingertips.

5. Teach Them to Succeed

It's one thing to teach someone how to use WordPress. It's another to teach them how to succeed with WordPress. Your training should go beyond simple mechanics and include best practices.

Yes, the title goes in the title field. But what makes an effective title? This is how you add an image, but here's how images can enhance your posts.

Make text bold like this, but here's how and why you'd want to do that (and when you shouldn't).

Yes, this is going beyond simple coding. It's really up to your client to use their website well. But you can help, even in a few small ways. And you should, because their success is your success.

WordPress Client Training Methods

There are several training methods you can use to bring your clients up to speed, each with their own pros and cons:

1. Documentation

One of the simplest ways to offer training is just to write out some documentation. There's plenty of source material out there, from the WordPress Codex[17] to other blogs and resources. Of course that means it's a source, not something you copy and paste. Make it your own.

There are several ways to deliver documentation, from an easily updated online source to something you print out and hand over.

While you can't update a physical copy, it is a tangible way to help that might be more comforting for clients who aren't tech savvy.

2. Videos

Training videos can be one of the best ways to show people how to use WordPress. A lot of people are visual learners and need to see it rather than read about it. It can also help to see things in action, see where to click and how things move.

---

17   http://codex.wordpress.org/

Plus, video is easy to outsource. There are several sources of white-label videos you can incorporate into your training.

The iThemes Toolkit comes with unbranded WordPress tutorial videos you can use to train your clients. It's easy to add slides or bumpers to the videos with your branding so they look even more professional. WP101 Plugin also offers training videos you can use and a plugin that allows you to make them part of the WordPress backend.

Even if you're not a video pro there are several ways you can train your clients with professional video.

3. Webinars

One of the most hands-on ways you can train your clients is with a personal webinar. Get online together and walk them through the site. This is going to be a big-time commitment for you, but it might be worth it, especially if you're dealing with a client who isn't comfortable with technology, or if you want to make a huge impression.

While you lose out on the time savings of pre-created resources, you get the benefit of full-service interaction, real-time questions and customization for the client.

While being live is a huge plus, it's also a downside. A webinar doesn't allow the client to refer back to anything later.

Make your webinar more effective by leaving something behind, whether it's full written documentation or even just an abbreviated cheat sheet.

4. Combination

If you're not sure about the best way to do WordPress client training, consider creating a combo of several of these methods. People learn in different ways, so it can be helpful to offer multiple options to your clients.

Pro Tip: Sandbox

One of the scary things about learning something new is messing it up. That pressure is even worse when you're talking about a live website. Even if you've done your job and made it hard for a client to mess up their own site, they still have that fear, and it can be crippling. If you've got a nervous client, ease their worries by giving them a sandbox site to play around with.

Because Coding Isn't Enough

WordPress client training is an important part of freelance development. Teaching people to use what you code will ensure you can go on coding. So make it part of your process. Bring your site development to a close with some solid customer service that will ensure everybody wins.

Selling Goods

As a freelancer you're likely selling your time. But what if you sold stuff? Creating and selling stuff is a big step forward in diversifying your income and joining the creator economy. We think it's something everyone should think about.

But if selling products isn't your primary business, why should you waste the time looking into it?

Why is selling something such a good idea for a freelancer?

Great question. We've got a whole bunch of reasons. Ready?

1. Creator Economy

Welcome to the creator economy. Gone are the days when people punch the clock and put in their hours at work. Now we create things. Now we work for ourselves. It's a massive shift in thinking.

Your primary source of income might be service based. You perform a service and get paid. But the creator economy means you can also create products based on your service and generate extra income. You can find a way to package what you do and boost your income potential.

The entrepreneurs in the room are drooling.

2. Move Beyond Your Limitations

You only have so many hours in the day. You can only rack up so many billable hours. There's a limit to how much money you can make. The income potential of your company is ultimately limited by people and hours.

Unless you sell products.

If you can find a way to package your service into a reproducible product, like an ebook or software, then you can move beyond those time-based limitations.

Selling stuff online can be like having a second job without having to put in the hours. You work the initial hours to create it, but then it keeps making money for you regardless of how many hours you put into it.

3. Think Like an Enterprise

Big, rich companies don't leave money on the table. They see the value in something and find a way to make money. You need to start thinking like an enterprise.

The stuff you create is valuable. You love it, so you don't want to think about it this way, but it's a commodity. Find a way to package it and charge money for it. All you're really doing is monetizing your assets.

Use some fancy business lingo if that works for you. But get on board. Make your assets work for you.

4. Income That Works For You

A big reason you should sell your own stuff is because it's an income stream that compliments everything else you do. If you accept advertising on your site you're ultimately pushing people away. If you do referral income with affiliates you're also pushing people away. These might be fine ways to make money, but they're income streams that work against you.

Instead of using your space, energy and effort to make money for other people, make money for yourself. Put that space and bandwidth into getting people to buy your own stuff. It keeps people engaged with you. It keeps them on your site and ultimately in your sphere. You're earning money and reinforcing your brand. Win, win.

5. Risk & Reward

If you want to make some money you're going to have to take some risks. Creating stuff involves a lot of risk. But there's also a lot of reward. Just ask Mark Zuckerberg or J.K. Rowling. It used to be that creating stuff required sharing the risk and reward with a publisher or other backer. Someone would share the risk with you to create whatever awesome idea you had. But in order to get that backing, you had to share the reward.

Publishers, record companies, producers and more gatekeepers got rich with this model. Some creators also got rich, but a lot of creators were deemed too risky. But today the Internet has made it possible to assume the risk yourself, or at least spread it among the crowd.

Author Hugh Howey found success on his own by selling his books in the Kindle Store. When the publishers came knocking he sold the print rights to his hit novel *Wool* but kept the digital rights for himself. The publisher couldn't offer anything he couldn't already do. The success of *Wool* was a big risk that Howey took on his own. Now he's keeping all the reward for himself, as it should be.

All the Kickstarter and Indiegogo projects flourishing today are an example of the risk being spread out. The giant gatekeepers aren't the only ones who can take on risk these days, and that means all the reward isn't locked up in their greedy fists. There's more reward for creators like you.

So the bottom line is you should create and sell something because the risk/reward model has been flipped upside down. There's not nearly as much risk to create your own stuff and the reward can be all yours.

6. Stability

It's a tough world out there. After the past few years we all know the nosedive the economy could take at any time. And no matter how well the economy is doing, you could still lose your job. You could lose that big client. Your traffic could disappear. You never know what's going to happen.

There's very little security out there.

Which is why it's important to take care of yourself. Cover your bases by having multiple income streams.

Selling a book probably isn't going to replace your salary, but it's a nice trickle that can provide some semblance of stability. When things start getting ugly, you're going to want every bit of stability you can get. It's a little extra to keep you going or stop the worries. It's an additional income stream that might give you the security to try something new or take a vacation.

7. Your Own Longtail

Nobody is reading your blog posts from 2009. But there's probably good stuff there. Just because it's five years old doesn't mean it's worthless. You could repackage it and help people rediscover it. Making content easy for people to find by repackaging it makes it worth paying for.

You should create something because it's an easy way to make the most of your content. In some ways it's even an environmental approach: **Reduce your work, reuse your stuff, recycle your income.**

And that's something everybody can do.

But I Have Nothing to Sell: Yes You Do

"But I have nothing to sell." That's the common excuse. You hear about ecommerce and you just shrug. Why should I pay attention, I don't have anything to sell? That's where you'd be wrong. Ecommerce can be for everybody because everybody has something to sell. You just might not realize it yet.

Oh, to be a developer these days. There are so many things yearning for good code, so many tasks longing to be simplified, so many options available with the proliferation of screens, WiFi and mobile. The work of a developer is no longer chained to a desk and an impersonal, immobile computer.

Plus, people are realizing that developers are cool: "I think people that make apps are artists," Will.i.am told Mashable "Power to the geeks."
[18]

There are so many things you can code for cash: apps, WordPress themes and plugins, snippets of code for various languages, add-ons and extensions for existing products, etc.
There are tons of options and different niches you can join.

Maybe your product isn't about code. If you can write, design or take pictures there are all kinds of opportunities. You could sell a book, a font or a stock photo. Don't be limited by your job title.

People have literally sold pixels online. You can sell anything.

All you need is a good idea, a vision for how it can take off and the determination to see it through.

---

18   http://mashable.com/2012/08/30/will-i-am-stem-mars/

Story: Products vs. Services

BASECAMP, TECH COMPANY

When thinking about selling products as a freelancer, it helps to find something you're already doing that you can repackage, repurpose or rework. You don't want to come up with a second job.

That's what happened with 37signals, the makers of Basecamp and other web-based software. They started out as a web development agency. They made websites for clients.

But being geeks, they created their own internal project management system. They needed something that worked the way they wanted it to, so they built it. When their clients got a glimpse of it, they wanted it too.

Basecamp was born.

Today they're not even called 37signals anymore. They changed their name to Basecamp. They scaled back the service-based client work and focused on subscription-based software products.

While they created great websites, it's clear their talents were wasted on client work. That kind of incredible success and fundamental shift in business model probably isn't going to happen for everybody. But it's possible.

Story: Selling Themes
CARRIE DILS, FREELANCE DEVELOPER

What have you learned from selling your own themes?

Oh goodness, I've learned a lot! Turns out that creating a theme takes the least amount of time. It's the mechanics of setting up a store, writing documentation, creating support channels, marketing and the like, that are so time-investment heavy. I don't say that to discourage anyone—there's still plenty of room in the market—but creating a theme for public release is a completely different prospect than whipping out a custom theme for a client. In addition to the rigors you put your code through, there are just a lot of other components involved.

I wrote a post about my experience selling themes that still stands.

I think the biggest thing I've learned since I wrote that is how much I still need to learn. Ha! I've been reading up lately on accessibility issues for WordPress and designing with a mobile user in mind first. I'm proud of the themes I've put out so far, but I look forward to making them even better the next time around.

Story: Moving up to Products

BRIAN CASEL, FREELANCE DESIGNER

How do you know when you're ready to level up?

For me it was kind of a growing frustration. I had left the agency and become a freelancer, and you have this freedom. After a few years I realized—how much freedom do I really have? I have all these clients, but I'm limited to what they want. Everybody knows how things go when working with clients who don't appreciate all the work you do or don't take your advice. That can become very frustrating after a while.

Then there was a frustration with selling my time for money. My income was tied to time. I was still charging per project, not hourly, but still I could only take on so many projects at one time. There was a ceiling to my income as a solo freelancer.

That's when I became motivated to scale up and build my team, get into products that would be more scalable and detached from my time.

Now I can earn an income in my sleep. Not that I sleep. I still work extremely hard. The income is scalable and the team grows.

Should all freelancers be leveling up to products?

I guess it's not necessarily for everybody. You might think moving to products means you're going to become a manager and in a lot of ways you are. But as I got into it, I found you can still use that creative energy in new ways.

You can still take all that creative energy you'd normally apply to pushing pixels in Photoshop and put it into designing efficient systems in your business or designing a really effective marketing website for a product.

I think it's important to push yourself into those areas that you might feel a little uncomfortable. That's really how you level up and grow.

I'm not in this to get huge. I'm very much of the bootstrap mindset.

I find making products and teaching—things that touch lots of people, rather than satisfying the whims of a few clients—to be much more enjoyable work.

Every day there's something new I learn. There are always things that are unexpected.

And that's the challenge and joy of freelancing. If a freelancer wants to transition to products, how should they get started?

Start small. Don't jump straight into doing software as a service (SaaS), don't get into building the next social network. **Start very small, and whatever you think is small, start even smaller than that.**

An ebook is a good example—write and sell an ebook. Or design a WordPress theme. Start by selling it in a marketplace just to get your feet wet with designing a product that is intended to be consumed by lots of people, rather than a website that's really only for one person or company.

That's a different beast, and it requires even more time and effort to make something for mass consumption (and mass could only mean 20 or 100 people).

You'll learn so much with the first product, so don't expect that to be your big thing that will consume you for 10 years. It won't. It might only be a project for the next six months. But the lessons will be incredibly valuable. Take those lessons into your second product, which will be a little bigger than the first.

Start small and take it one step at a time.

Marketing

No big surprise: you need to market yourself. If you want to be successful as a freelancer, you can't just sit there and wait for the work to come in.

You need to communicate who you are, what you do and build trust that you can deliver and follow through. That can happen in a number of different ways, including networking, branding, business cards, websites, social media and lots more.

The fact is, you're doing marketing whether you intend to or not. Sitting at home and refusing to spread the word is a kind of marketing (really bad marketing). So put some thought into it. Be intentional. Think about how you want to come across to potential clients, how you want to be seen, how you might connect.

Then do it.

Branding

Branding is the soul of your business. It's more than a logo or stationary, it's the emotional connection that people make with your product or service. You need to define and develop your brand.

Why Do You Need Branding?

You may be thinking you're just a lonely freelancer and don't need a fancy brand. After all, you're not Apple or Harley Davidson.

Wrong.

There's more competition than ever before. There's a bigger global market.

There are more people setting out on their own and doing exactly what you are.

Fortunately there are also more clients than ever, but they need to be able to find you. You need to stand out. You can't get lost in the background of boring, faceless companies. You need to give people something to latch on to, something to connect with and remember who you are and why they should do business with your company. Branding can deliver that.

You also need a brand because you'll be branded anyway. If you don't offer something, then people will make up their own mind about you. You'll get labeled anyway, so you might as well make it a good label.

What's Your Story?

Great brands have a great story. It communicates something. It gets to the heart of who you are and what you value and what you offer. It's an image that communicates quickly, a visual shorthand for what you're about. What's your story?

Your brand will help you stand out from the crowd, so don't be afraid to be creative. Come up with something interesting, engaging and memorable. Technical work is often perceived as boring and mundane, so this is an opportunity to flip expectations and surprise people. And when people are surprised, you've succeeded.

Creating a Brand

Ultimately your brand is more than a logo and a color scheme. It's more than an identity package. It's the personality of your company and how you uniquely serve your clients.

You create your brand by thinking through specifics of your personality:

- What's your style? Are you corporate and straight-laced or are you laid-back and casual?

- What's your voice? Are you commanding and professional or are you friendly and personal?

- What's your look? Are you refined and clean or are you grunge and chaotic?

Sometimes it's easier to come up with your brand by asking how you'd respond in different situations:

- How would you celebrate a milestone? Maybe a party for your clients? What kind of party? Or would you send your clients a gift? What kind of gift—something funny or useful? Or would a celebration not even be appropriate—you're too focused on business to stop to celebrate.

- How would you react to a public mistake? Mistakes happen, but how you respond is up to you. Would you issue a formal apology and make amends? Or would you craft a humorous apology that pokes fun at yourself while moving forward?

- Say you were wrapping a car in advertising—what kind of a car would you want? Something fun and hip like a VW Beatle? Something tough and rugged like a Hummer? Maybe something sporty and sleek like a Corvette or practical like a Toyota Prius.

These kinds of questions and scenarios can help you see how a brand would play out and help you determine what brand will work best for your freelance business.

This is a quick overview of branding, but there are loads of resources out there to help you understand branding and create your own. **Tip:** Branding is far more than business cards, but make sure you have them. Far too often in a crucial moment someone asks for a card and you're empty handed. That's no good. Once you've nailed down your branding and designed some cards, order a crate of them and stick stacks of them everywhere—in your wallet or purse, your bag, your glove box, wherever you can stick them. Make sure you never run out.

We'll talk more about business cards soon.

Personal vs. Business Branding

A big branding issue to consider is whether you want a personal or business brand. There are pros and cons to both:

Personal Brand
- Will always stay with you, wherever you go.
- Can be easier for a freelancer because you're selling "you."
- Can establish stronger emotional connections.
- Can be easier to build and maintain long term.
- Can seem "smaller" and more personal than company brands.

One of the biggest issues with a personal brand is if you'll ever want to sell your business. It's not easy to sell your personal name. In many ways the business lives and dies with you.

Also, if you want to grow as a company and bring in employees, a personal brand can have limitations (though it is possible to transition to a business brand).

Business Brand

- Can be built, sold and transferred.
- Allow you to hide behind them (to a degree).
- Can appear more professional to certain clients.
- Can take longer to build but may offer more stability.
- Can be created to be more memorable.

If you want a company that goes outside of what you can personally do or offer, then you should create a business brand name and not use your own name.

Story: Name

JUSTIN SAINTON, FREELANCE DEVELOPER, ZAO

A lot of freelancers name their companies after themselves. Can you tell us about the name Zao and why you didn't name the company after yourself?

The name was kind of a dual focus. It's a Greek word and Chinese word. I spent a year in China when I was 14 and 15. In Greek it means living water. I became a Christian when I was 16, so it was an important part of that process.

From the beginning I never intended Zao to be just myself. I never had any desire to be JustinSainton.com or even Justin Design Group or whatever. I always had the vision of building something that could outlive myself. Even from 16 and 17 on I had this idea of legacy. The legacy I want to leave, the legacy I want to build.

As a 16-year-old I thought what are my grandkids' grandkids' grandkids going to know about me and how are they going to be affected by me?

> How do I build for that today? Justin Sainton Media Group — that was never a way to build that legacy. So that was part of the company brand.
>
> **Wow. How many 16-year-olds are thinking about legacy?**
>
> I don't know. I know guys in their 60s who don't think that way, so I don't know if it's experience or what. I've been living away from my parents since I was 15, so you have to grow up a little quicker, you have to think longer term. For me that was a big part of coming into Christianity. It's how I see God thinking—he's a very long-term thinker. Some of it was rooted in that. To be honest, I don't really know.

Narrow Your Focus

An important part of branding is narrowing your focus and making it clear what you do.

You can't do everything. You can't serve everybody.

Lexus and Toyota serve two different audiences (though they're part of the same company). They offer different products and communicate differently to two different audiences.

So a helpful early step in marketing yourself as a freelancer is to narrowly define your client.

What type of client are you looking for? What's your niche? Narrow the field so you know what you're looking for and who you're going after. Then start to specifically define them. What type of business are they? What are they looking for? Where would they spend their free time? By defining your client you can begin to think like your client and you'll be able to find them, pitch to them and land them.

So you need to get very specific about what you do. But you also need to communicate in everyday language. Don't use coding jargon.

That can be a tall order. Here's how to make it simple:

- "Web Developer" – Too broad. What's your specialty?
- "I specialize in SASS." – What? Avoid the acronyms. Use English.
- "I build WordPress sites for small businesses." — There you go. Much better.

Even the above example could be narrowed further—what kind of small businesses? What industries? Located where?

The more you can narrow your focus and define your audience, the easier it is to do marketing.

Story: Narrow Your Focus
JUSTIN SAINTON, FREELANCE DEVELOPER, ZAO

What have you found to be the most effective way to bring in business?

For me the most effective method has really been focus. Honestly, those first two years, even four years, I was very generalized. I could do anything and everything and I was OK at it. I wasn't known for anything.

But now I have all this background in ecommerce. That was one of the first projects we did. I really started focusing on WordPress and ecommerce. I contributed to WP eCommerce. I contributed to some open source projects. I became known in the community as an ecommerce guy, so when someone needs an ecommerce project they know who to go to.

The number one way to bring in business is to focus on something. If I say I'm a plugin developer or a theme designer, well everybody develops plugins and makes themes. If you need a high scale ecommerce website or custom work for WP eCommerce, or you're having trouble with a caching strategy for an ecommerce plugin—even in that specific focus, there are guys like Daniel Espinoza for ecommerce or Curtis McHale if you need a membership site. Even just focusing within the focus, becoming well known for a niche has been helpful.

So figure out what you want to focus on and become the absolute best at it. It could be as general as a go-to guy for low-level ecommerce, or I want to be the expert for WooCommerce membership sites that use PayPal. Build and position yourself. Focus.

Focus on systems, on personal disciplines, on your business—focus in general is huge.

Corporate Communication

A big part of your marketing effort is corporate communication. This is how you communicate not just to your clients, but the wider public. This can include all kinds of things, such as email newsletters, websites, social media, press releases and more—some of which we'll cover in more detail.

Toot Your Own Horn

Sometimes it's hard for people to talk about themselves. They don't want to be too overtly promotional or be seen as bragging. Well, you need to learn to toot your own horn. If you won't talk about your own successes, why would anybody else?

Ken Blanchard brought this point home when we said "If you don't toot your own horn once in a while, somebody is liable to use it for a spittoon."

Where you land on this will depend on your branding, but no matter the approach you take you're going to need to get over it and promote yourself. If you're uncomfortable with it maybe you take a more laid-back approach. But if you want business, it needs to be done.

Don't Go Dark

No matter how you decide to communicate, don't go dark. You should always be visible and responsive in whatever channels you choose to communicate.

- If you opened a Twitter account or a Facebook page, keep it current. Nothing says 'lame' like a six-month-old feed.
- If you've got a blog, update it frequently. There's no sense having one if you're not going to keep it updated.
- If you have email addresses, be sure you're monitoring what comes in and responding to new leads in a timely manner.
- If you make your phone number public, be sure you actually answer it or have a professional voice mail. And call people back. It's simple courtesy and professionalism.

Know What People Are Saying

Set up Google alerts for your company's name and your own name so you know what people are saying. Be on the watch so you can respond to problems or thank people for saying nice things. It's part of being responsive and protecting your reputation.

Story: Marketing Funnel

KEVIN D. HENDRICKS, FREELANCE WRITER, MONKEY OUTTA NOWHERE

One of the most helpful things I learned about marketing my freelance business was the idea of a marketing funnel. It's a simple concept that helped me envision the reality of marketing and how to be effective.

Basically all your marketing efforts are like dumping leads into a funnel. It's wide at the top and narrow at the bottom. Your marketing work—networking, email newsletters, website, social media, etc.—goes in the top. Paying projects come out the bottom.

You have to put in a lot at the top to get out a little at the bottom. And if you stop doing the work at the top of the funnel—if you let your website grow stale, go quiet on social media or stop attending networking events—the you'll have even fewer projects coming out at the bottom.

I found this so helpful because it reminded me I have to keep working on my marketing, even if I don't see results. It also reminded me that it's not a balanced system. The work I put into marketing is not going to equal the projects I get from it. I might have to put in 10 times the effort on my marketing.

Of course it's not a perfect analogy. Whatever you put into a real funnel eventually comes out the bottom. That's not true with a marketing funnel. Apparently it's a leaky funnel. You can try to plug the holes with a stronger pitch, emphasizing benefits and reaching the right audience, but you still won't have a 100% success rate.

In fact, a 5% success rate is often considered great in typical marketing.

> Consider the reality of that as you're toiling on websites, emails and more. 95% of people will see your marketing and move on. That can be depressing. But focus on getting enough people to see your marketing that only 5% of those will keep you busy.

Business Cards

The age old business card is still key to connecting with potential clients.

- It's something tangible you can pass out.
- It makes it easy for people to remember who you are.
- It paves the way for future contact.
- Trading business cards greases the wheels of that first interaction.
- Bonus: Loads of places collect business cards in a fish bowl for random drawings for free goods. They're only trying to solicit you, but hey, free stuff! Plus you can always turn the tables and make your own pitch.

People have their own process for handling contacts and it almost always includes business cards. If you don't fit in their process, you'll be forgotten.

Your Name Here

Since we're focusing on personal contact, your name should be the most important (and therefore biggest) thing on your card. Your company name is secondary. People form a relationship with you, not your company. So unless you work for Apple or some other major company that has a name that will open doors for you, make your name the biggest thing on your card.

It's not about ego, it's about connecting with you. You need them to remember your name more than anything. So make it big.

Contact Info

Next you need the appropriate information on your card. There's a temptation to load up your card with every form of contact information possible—but that's not helpful. Put in the most important details and leave the rest off.

Think about your ideal clients. What are the most common ways they'll use to contact you? Make sure you include that information on your card. Unless a local address is important to you, people probably don't need your mailing address.

Tip: Set up a Google voice number that will forward people to your preferred phone, whether it's your cell phone, your business line or your home number.

Some Other Business Card Elements You May Want to Consider:

Funnel Statement

Your business card should help make it clear what you do and why the potential client needs you. This should be a short statement—maybe 15 words or less—that summarizes what you do. It's more than a tagline but shorter than an elevator pitch. This is important so people will remember who you are and why they should follow up with you.

Spend some time on this. Do some free writing with no word limits to get down exactly what you do. Then rewrite it in half as many words. Then do it again.

Keep halving it until you get down to 15 words or less. That's your funnel statement. Slap it on your business cards.

Even if you don't include it on your business card, it's an extremely helpful exercise to go through to help *you* become crystal clear about what you do and who you work with.

Include an Offer

Consider adding some sort of extra offer to your business card. Include something that will intrigue people and make them check out your website or drop you a line.

- Maybe you have a free ebook available on your site—pitch it on your business card.
- Maybe it's some kind of deal like 10% off.
- Maybe it's a free site evaluation or SEO check—something of value that's simple for you to provide.

It's an opportunity to do a little more and give people that extra reason to hang on to your card.

Blank Space

Finally, include some blank space on your cards. Some experts recommend leaving the entire back of your business card empty (while others might say to put your funnel statement here).

Leaving the back blank gives people room to write on your business card. A lot of people use this strategy to take notes or jot down extra details they want to remember. You want to encourage a contact to do that—if they want to write something down about you then they'll be more likely to become a customer. You should encourage that behavior!

Blank space on your cards also gives you an opportunity. It always happens at events that someone forgets their cards or runs out.

You can step in with your own card and ask them to write their information down for you on the back of your card. That way you still get their information and you come across as the hero.

Website

In today's digital age a website is the storefront for any freelance website developer. Without a site, you basically don't exist. You need a website.

C'mon. You're web developers. You know this stuff. It's the same pitch you give to those backward clients who still want phonebook ads.

Of course you already have a freelance website pitching your skills. Please. But is it working? Is your website doing you any good? It's easy for your site to fall to the bottom your to-do list.

Simply put: **You're too busy building awesome sites for your clients to have an awesome site yourself.**

That's a problem. Let's talk about how to fix your website.

Why You Need a Freelance Website

Before we get too far, let's remember why you even need a freelance site. You know the website pitch—you give it all the time. But there's a problem. Traditionally we say the cobbler's children have no shoes.

Web developers frequently have the same problem. Or you have a website—it was easy to build an awesome website in your early days when you weren't busy. But your site gets older and crustier with each year that goes by. Not cool.

If you're trying to sell yourself as a builder of websites, then you better have a website for yourself. And it probably shouldn't suck.

Here's why you need a freelance website that works:

- **Bring in Business** – Your site should be a continual pipeline of new business. You might not need new business today, but who knows what will happen down the road (or, you know, next week). Those referrals could dry up and you'll be in trouble. So keep that marketing funnel full with a solid freelance website.

- **Establish Credibility** – We've been at this Internet game for a while now, but there's still that pesky question of credibility. Anyone can set up a site and claim they're an amazing developer. But having a solid freelance website gives you a chance to prove your credibility with quality content, social proof, in-bound search and more.

- **Home Base** – With all the social media options and portfolio platforms, it's tempting to abandon your freelance website. But those sites will come and go. You need a solid home base to serve as your online hub.

- **SEO Goodness** – You want people to find you online, especially when they search for your name or your town and "web developer." Good search engine optimization (SEO) only happens with a good freelance website.

Web Is Not #1

Now let's be realistic. Your freelance website is probably not your primary source for clients. Other avenues for potential leads are arguably more important than your freelance website. But you still need a site.

A freelance website is the foundation that makes word of mouth, email, social and every other channel more effective.

Your website is an anchor to bring in new business. Those word of mouth referrals will go to your website to contact you. Those Twitter followers will check out your website to learn more about you. Any email campaign is going to push people to your site.

Seeing the trend? Your website is central for incoming leads. You can't keep pushing it to the bottom of your to-do list.

How to Make Your Own Site Happen

OK, OK—we've all fallen victim to the cobbler's shoe problem. But what do you do? How do you make your website a priority?

Remember the Importance

The first thing you need to do is accept how important it is. **We all know how important a website is, but you need to remind yourself.** We allow our excuses to dilute this truth and we keep pushing it off. Meanwhile our crusty site gets even worse and those leads click the contact button less frequently.

Put It on Your Calendar

Making your own stuff a priority requires carving out the time. You need to literally put it on your calendar. This should be part of a regular effort to work on your own business, creativity and skill.

Outsource Your Site

It may feel like cheating to outsource your own site, but it's a legitimate way to get it done. Maybe you just outsource the portions you don't like doing—the writing, the graphic design, the grunt work.

You tell your clients to bring in professionals all the time, so why not do it yourself?

Just because it's your freelance website doesn't mean you can't get help to create it.

Scale Back Your Plans

You also tell your clients to scale back their dreams when they're being too unrealistic. It's OK to do the same thing yourself. Maybe you don't have time to build the freelance website of your dreams. But instead of putting it off, create something smaller. Start small and work up to the site of your dreams. **Some progress is better than no progress.**

What Your Website Must Have

So you've come to terms with the importance of your freelance website and you've found a way to make it happen. Now what do you need to do to make it better?

Let's start with the basics. Here's what your site needs to have:

Contact Page

Yes, people need to be able to get in touch with you. Duh. Do we really need to mention this? Yeah, we do. Because listing contact info alone isn't good enough.

- Make sure your contact info is accessible from every page. If you don't put the info itself on every page, make sure it's in the menu on every page.
- Think through your strategy: How do you want people to contact you? Phone, email, web form? How do you process each of those requests? Make sure you have a system in place.

- If you're brave enough to post your email address, consider steps to minimize spam.
- If you're using a contact form, consider that every field will lower your response rate. Do you really need a prospective client's mailing address? Keep it simple. And test that contact form!
- Consider giving people options. A web form may be the best way to contact you, but some people like to pick up the phone.

Portfolio

Your freelance website needs to show off your work. You should have an online portfolio so potential contacts can always check out your stuff. We'll talk in more detail about a portfolio, but for now just make sure it's part of your website.

Credibility

Anybody can have a website. What makes you credible? Your freelance website is an opportunity to back up your claims. This is a chance to tout who you are and show off your portfolio. Give some client quotes or brag about your WordPress contributions.

You could also point to what you do as a way to back up what you say. Any content marketing that shows your expertise, such as a blog, podcast, tutorial video, etc., will do nicely.

You could also point to exterior sources such as social media. If you've got a big following on Twitter and are routinely talking about your business, featuring your Twitter account can be a good way to establish credibility.

Nitty Gritty Benefits

Your homepage needs to give that big picture, an easily understandable statement of what you do. But as you dive into your freelance website, you need to give more details about what you can deliver. This is where you explain your services.

But don't give us a list of what you do. Talk about how what you do can benefit customers. This is the classic features vs. benefits distinction. Apple talks benefits when they say 1,000 songs, while Microsoft focuses on features when they say 4 GB.

Brian Casel[19] says it well:

"Most freelancers' sites need to be less about you, (the freelancer), and more about the customer. They really need to speak more to their ideal client and communicate the benefits that client is going to receive from choosing to work with the freelancer. Rather than saying, 'I design websites and I love to use WordPress,' say something more along the lines of, 'You can grow your business and manage your own website using WordPress, and I'm here to make it easy.' That's the angle you want."

What You Must Have

Those are some basics your freelance website must have: contact info, portfolio, credibility and specific benefits. Everybody needs those. But what's going to make your freelance website stand out?

Ways to Make Your Freelance Website Work

Now that your website has the basics that everybody needs, what can you do to stand out from the crowd and be effective?

Content Marketing

A powerful one-two punch is to show your expertise and deliver something helpful. Content marketing does both.

---

19   http://ithemes.com/2014/08/06/web-designer-brian-casel-offers-advice-freelancers/

Whether you're blogging, creating tutorials, doing a podcast, hangout or something else, it showcases your skills and helps people out.

Not only does content display your expertise, but it also serves as an introduction to potential clients.

"The best clients I get have actually sat down and read a bunch of my website," says web developer Curtis McHale[20]. "They get to feel like they know me—there are no surprises."

Your website can actually pave the way for a good working relationship.

Just make sure your content marketing is current. There's nothing worse than seeing a blog that hasn't been updated in months. If you can't commit to keeping it current, then don't do it.

For more on content creation:

Grab our free *Blogging Isn't Dead*[21] and *15 Best Practices for Rockin' Webinars ebooks*[22].

Give Back

Another way to stand out is by giving back. Content marketing is one way to give back, but you might do less public efforts, like contributing to the WordPress community with code, upgrades, plugins, volunteering by planning a meetup or other efforts.

---

20   https://ithemes.com/2014/06/13/freelance-wordpress-developer-curtis-mchale/

21   http://ithemes.com/publishing/blogging-isnt-dead-ebook/

22   http://ithemes.com/publishing/15-best-practices-for-rockin-webinars/

The downside, of course, is these efforts are less public. So you'll need to find ways to make sure these things are reflected on your website. You want these things to speak for themselves, not look like a self-serving pat on the back.

For more on how to give back:

Take a look at our free *How to Run a WordPress Meetup*[23] ebook.

Stats

Make sure your website has Google Analytics or some other stat system installed. Yes, this is no brainer stuff—but remember the cobbler's shoes—stats are a tool you might put off or overlook.

Dig into your stats and see what pages are working and which ones aren't.

For more on stats:

Check out our free ebook, *Getting Started With Google Analytics*[24].

Your Website Should Win

It's not always your first love. But your freelance website should be awesome. Carve out the time to make it work. It will be well worth the investment.

---

23   http://ithemes.com/publishing/run-wordpress-meetup/

24   http://ithemes.com/publishing/getting-started-with-google-analytics/

Story: Content

CARRIE DILS, FREELANCE DEVELOPER

What have you found to be the most effective at bringing in business?

In the past, customer referrals were always my biggest source of new business. There's no better referral than the one I get from a happy client!

A couple of years ago I made a concerted effort to generate more content on my site (tutorials, DIY blog posts, etc.), and that's led to a tremendous increase in what I call "stranger referrals"—people I have no connection to. At present, I generate over 60% of my business from total strangers who've discovered me online. I'm not a blogging mastermind or business guru, but I've been amazed at what a consistent online presence has accomplished for my business.

How do you find the balance between contributing to the community with tutorials, podcasts, etc., and getting distracted from work that pays the bills?

This is such a great question and something I struggle to find balance with. Although the time/resources I give to the community don't net direct profit, I know they've increased my exposure over time, which leads back to those "stranger referrals." In that way, continuing to contribute is selfishly important. Of course, I love it too. At the risk of being ridiculous for quoting myself, I frequently say, "It's more fun to solve someone else's problem than work on my own".

The Genesis Office Hours podcast is taking more and more of my time, but I absolutely love doing it. I'm considering sponsorship and some other ways to re-coup some of that time. We'll see what happens!

Email List

Everybody talks about collecting an email list these days, and that can be an important way to capture potential customers and make sure you can reach out to them again.

But be careful what you promise with an email list.

Collecting email addresses and never sending anything to them is doomed to failure. If you only send an email once a year—or whenever you think of it—your open rates will plunge and your spam rates will skyrocket. Nobody will remember signing up for your email, and they won't read it. Big waste of everybody's time.

Just like content marketing, **an email list needs to be current and consistent**. You need to create a plan for producing content and a consistent schedule for sending out updates. And you have to stick with it.

Your emails can be short. All it needs to be is a quick check-in with potential clients and offer something of value. Don't turn your email into a giant monstrosity you'll never be able to keep up with. Make it manageable.

Limit the frequency to something you can handle as well. A monthly email isn't very often, but that's still 12 times per year. Do you have enough content for 12 updates every year? Even a quarterly email is better than just sending it randomly. A random email is a good way to fail.

Portfolio

Potential clients want to see that you can actually build the stuff you claim you can. They want proof. A portfolio is an ideal way to show the type and quality of work you can deliver.

Many freelancers get consistent work based solely on the strength of their portfolio. Let your past work do the talking.

Make It Portable

Your portfolio should be portable. Definitely put it on your website. That should be the default location.

But you also might want a version saved on your favorite device so you can show it off while you're on the go. You never know when you'll be talking to a potential client but not have Internet access—or be forced to rely on someone else's spotty Internet connection. Plus, having a version saved on your device means it will load speedy fast.

You also might want to have a printed version ready to go so you can pull it out at a moment's notice.

How Big Should My Portfolio Be?

"Don't just list everything you've ever worked on in your portfolio," says web designer Brian Casel. "Pick three to five really great projects that represent the type of work you want to get."

Half a dozen amazing pieces in your portfolio is better than a dozen good pieces. **Be picky.**

What Should My Portfolio Include?

Clients should see themselves in your portfolio, so don't pick extreme examples that are outside your normal work.

And wowing your clients isn't the point. Each example in your portfolio should showcase how you solved a client's problem, as Brian suggests:

"Don't just use screenshots. Put up case studies. Include testimonials: their problem and what solution you delivered. That shows the customer how they can benefit from what you offer."

Not only does this make a better case to potential clients, but it's also good for search engine optimization (SEO).

Are Links Enough?

No. It's not enough to link to a site you designed. As Brian suggests above, you should talk about the project, what the client needed and how you delivered. You should have screenshots and then link to the site if it's still live and working. You should check periodically to make sure those links still work. If they don't or the site has changed, update your portfolio (and check in with the client).

What If I'm Not Proud of Them?

If you're not proud of the work you have to show, put it out there anyway. Having nothing to show is worse. Plus, everybody starts somewhere.

Then your top priority is to replace the crappy projects with better ones. Keep doing this as you, your skill and your experience grow.

What If I Have No Projects to Show?

Get some. If you're just starting out and don't have a portfolio, there are a couple of ways you can remedy this—and it will help build your experience, knowledge and confidence. You can design some sites pro bono, perhaps selecting a nonprofit or two that need a new site. But be clear about what's included in the site design so it doesn't get out of hand. It's just as important to be clear about contract boundaries with pro bono clients as it is paying clients.

Or design sample sites that showcase your skills. Develop different types of sites emphasizing different design techniques. Be honest about them being sample sites – it still shows the quality of work you can deliver. This, in turn, develops your experience, knowledge and confidence, even before you've had a paying client.

Contribute to an Open Source Project

A simple way to market yourself as a freelance web designer is to contribute to an open source project. It blends learning and networking while creating a project to show off. So it's a triple win.

Find an open source project you're interested in and get involved in the community around it. If you can't find one, simply release something cool you've built and build interest around your own project.

Your work on open source projects can become part of your portfolio, plus it shows that you can work with others in a collaborative environment.

Here are some more questions for evaluating an open source project to contribute to:

- Is it something you're passionate about?
- How big and active is the community around it?
- Do other people care about it?
- Does it leverage your skills?
- Does it stretch you and your skills?
- Are you able to expand your contacts and relationships?
- Will your work be visible to show others?

Prove Your Skills

Another bonus to working on an open source project is it proves your skill to the community.

Your code is live and public for the world to see, and your colleagues can check it out and see what kind of coder you are.

For WordPress developer Andrew Norcross, that's the first question he asks in a job interview. Why? Because public code communicates a lot about a developer:

"First off, it shows they are involved with the community at some level. But in detail, it gives me insight into the person as a developer. Do they follow best practices? Do they cut corners? If there's enough code to review, has their skill set grown? These are things you can't get in a verbal interview."

Story: Giving Back

BILL ERICKSON, FREELANCE DEVELOPER

You've given back a lot to the WordPress community, including core contributions and plugins. How has that helped your business?

The biggest way I've given back is with tutorials and code snippets. A lot of people with WordPress problems will Google how to fix it and find my stuff. Even if they aren't technical enough to use it, they see my name over and over again, and they realize they should hire me when they're ready for a developer. That's helped. Plugins are less effective, they don't drive traffic and clients, but it's a value add to clients. When I build functionality for a client, it could be frozen in time or we could release it as a plugin, where it will get better and improve over time as I develop and others contribute. That's free improvements for the client.

My Display Posts Shortcode plugin is an example. A client did dog food reviews and they wanted to make lists to query different things, such as dog food reviews for dogs with diabetes or gluten free food. I wrote a short code to do it. Then I generalized it and released it. Now it's been downloaded nearly 80,000 times and included in WordPress.com. It's been improved by the WordPress code audit team, and I'm still improving it.

All of this, 90% of the features, the client didn't pay for. He paid for 10%. Yet he gets the benefit from it, and so does the community in general. If I just leave that functionality in your site and don't roll out a plugin, it's frozen. No one maintains it. But if I turn it into a plugin, more people get the benefit and it gets better with age.

Ninety percent of the time I don't have a plugin to spinout, so it's not in the initial contract. But when I build it, I ask the client if I can spend extra time and make it a public plugin and we'll talk about it. It creates more value for everyone in the process.

Finding Clients

All this marketing work is ultimately about finding clients. That's the goal: connect with people and close a sale.

Let's get more specific about connecting with potential clients as part of your marketing efforts.

The first step is to **build contacts**. These are people you know and can reach out to. You may not be best buds, but you have their contact info and with a quick memory jog they would remember you ("We met at that business breakfast last week." "Oh yeah, I remember. How's it going?").

It sure beats cold calling strangers.

The first step is to turn strangers into contacts.

The second step is to turn those contacts into clients with contracts.

It's a two-step process, and much like the marketing funnel, you're going to need a lot of contacts to get just a few who turn into clients.

So let's talk more about how to get contacts and turn them into contracts.

Philosophy

Contacts don't just fall into your lap. You have to work to get them. But we have a few ideas and ways to think about soliciting contacts that will make it seem less like work and more like everyday life.

No Cold Calls

Nobody likes making cold calls and nobody likes getting them. It's a low return approach and it's demoralizing. Don't do it. There's a better approach that's more natural, more effective and more personal.

It's called being human.
Building a personal relationship with somebody is the best way to form a contact and then turn that contact into a client.

This entire approach is based on the idea that people want to do business with people they know and trust. They want a relationship, not a stiff stranger cold calling. So what do you do? You meet people. You talk. You get to know them. You form an actual relationship. Then when you ask for their business, it's no longer a cold call. Or better yet, they come to you.

Quantity vs. Quality

As you're trying to develop contacts and get clients, remember that quality is better than quantity. This isn't some numbers game. **You don't win by collecting the most business cards.** Instead you want to walk away with a few names of people you really connected with, quality leads that have potential to be future clients.

Take the time to invest in people. It will pay off.

That said, quantity still has its place. You can't rely on just two or three freelance relationships to keep your business going. You need to develop a lot of relationships. Very few of those relationships are going to turn into paying gigs, so you need a lot of them.

Focus on developing quality connections every day and eventually you'll have the quantity you need. Nobody said you can't have both.

Attitude

Is this going to devolve into some kind of *How to Make Friends* weirdness? No, we'll spare you from that. But your attitude has a big influence on making connections and finding clients.

You need the right attitude to make freelance friends. The end product clearly matters, but what process do your clients have to go through to get there? **Nobody wants to work with a jerk.** Is working with you a chore? Are you always negative? Nobody wants to listen to complaints all the time.

Do you know those people who light up a room? They always have something good to say. They're always making people laugh. They're known as team players and contributors. Everybody wants to be their friend.

That's the kind of attitude that will open doors.

Now not everyone has that kind of a magical personality. We can't all light up the room. But we can work to make a good impression.

- **Be nice:** Don't whine or complain.
- **Be personable:** Ask about other people and don't just talk about yourself.
- **Listen:** Don't interrupt and don't monopolize the conversation.
- **Be confident:** But you also need to speak up and contribute.
- **Be polite:** Never badmouth other people.
- **Be positive and inspiring:** Encourage other people's ideas and inspire them to do more.

This is pretty basic stuff. But a bad attitude is going to lose you clients.

Serve Don't Sell

Instead of always trying to sell people, find ways to do something for people. **Find ways you can meet other people's needs.** Recommend other freelancers, suggest articles or books that might helpful, make an introduction to someone in their field.

Be of service to other people, not just another salesperson.

This approach will open lots of doors. People will be grateful for your help and they'll remember it. They'll be likely to return the favor. If you want to build relationships, you need to help people out.

Want to be remembered? Meet someone's need. They'll remember how you helped long after they've tossed everyone else's business cards.

Show Respect

When you meet new people, show some respect. Listen intently and ask questions. Try to remember their name. Don't be disinterested or aloof.

When they hand you their business card, read it. Don't just shove it in your pocket—write something on it and follow up later. That's perhaps the biggest thing you can do—show the people you meet that you're serious. Reach out to them later, even if it's just to follow them on Twitter or say hello. You'll make an impression and they'll know you're not just another random handshake.

Practical Ideas to Find Clients

In order to get contacts you need to get out there. It's tough to meet new people if you stay in your office all day. Hiding behind your computer is not an effective relationship-building strategy. And, while showing off the stellar websites you've designed is one way of marketing your business, you need to spend as much time working *on* your business as working *in* your business.

Free Training

A great way to meet people is to create your own opportunities. Offer free training classes through local libraries, business networks, community education, churches, etc. Do a simple training on how to blog or how to set up a WordPress site. Depending on the location and the setup, offer a 45-minute training and then give a five-minute pitch at the end for your services. Lawyers, realtors and insurance agents have been doing this for years, and you can too.

Make up fliers about the class and hang them wherever you can, from community bulletin boards to the coffee shop. Be sure any promotion you do for the class includes your website.

Offer a handout that includes an outline of your course and your website. Stay after to answer questions and engage with people. Have plenty of business cards on hand and pass them out.

While your primary audience here is the people who show up for the class, you can also reach people who see your class advertised and people referred by someone who attended your class. Don't underestimate the "Grandma" who seems like an unlikely WordPress student. Even if she's slow to catch on, she may know people in need of your services and be more than happy to recommend you.

Tip: Libraries are ideal for free training. Offer your classes in the evening to be more accommodating to business owners.

Local Search

The location-based services and local search can be a goldmine for finding contacts. Use a location based-search and look for local stores and businesses near you. You might find businesses within walking distance that you didn't even know were there.

Do a little research on their needs. Check out their online listings, visit their website, Google them—figure out what you might be able to offer. Then take a walk and introduce yourself. Small businesses like to work with local businesses and there's no better pitch than offering to fill a need.

Tip: While you're doing local search, you should also make sure your business is listed so other folks can find you.

Local Business Events

There are tons of local networking opportunities, from casual meetups to organized conferences to hanging out in the local coffee shop where other business people and freelancers hang out. Attend a few in your area and get to know people. The great thing about going to actual networking events is that people attend specifically to meet people. So it's not awkward when you pull out your business card or walk up to a stranger and introduce yourself.

There are tons of different events, but here are a few places to start:

- Local chamber of commerce: See what kind of events they host or sponsor.
- Local associations: What events or conferences do they host?
- Search "tweetup" and your city to find local social media gatherings.
- Check out local WordCamps or other WordPress meetups.

Tip: If you're especially nervous, go with a friend. Together you can tag team it and you won't have to stand around alone.

Friends & Family

Networking with friends and extended family can lead to greater opportunities. In many cases the contact may not be your cousin, but your cousin's boss (and it may just be your cousin after all, so don't overlook any opportunity).

An easy way to start with your family and friends is to be proactive about your services:

- Your sister mentions a side project knitting and selling scarves. You could recommend developing a website that allows people to preorder.
- A friend announces they're starting the adoption process. You could encourage them to start a blog to record the process and share the journey with family and friends.
- Your brother-in-law coaches little league. Suggest he launch a team website with practice times, location and other information parents will want.

But as you begin working with family and friends—be careful!
You should always charge something so your family and friends understand the value of your work. Sure, give them a huge discount, but still charge them something.

You'll save yourself headaches when a free project gets out of hand.

These projects may not be huge moneymakers for you, but they will powerfully demonstrate your skills to your family and friends. In turn, they'll start talking up your skills and recommending you to people you'd otherwise never meet. It also helps build up your portfolio.

Job Boards

The Internet is full of job boards with people looking for the skills you can offer. Browse through some listings and you might find your next gig. While these listings generally cater to one-off jobs, each one is an opportunity to form a relationship and build long-lasting clients and referrals for more business.

Some of these listings will be flooded with low-ball offers, so watch out for jobs that just aren't worth your time. Don't compete with someone working for much less than they should be (often high school students or overseas workshops).

General Tech Boards

In some cases you may need to search for "WordPress" or other keywords to narrow the results to something relevant.

- jobs.smashingmagazine.com
- authenticjobs.com
- getacoder.com
- krop.com
- odesk.com
- simplyhired.com

WordPress Specific Boards

These sites specializing in WordPress will offer even more specific listings.

- Customyze.me
- wphired.com
- jobs.wordpress.net
- wordpressfreelance.com
- premium.wpmudev.org/wpmu-jobs
- jobs.woothemes.com

Other Boards & Sites

- WPCandy.com/pros – Their professional listing section might be a good place to set up a profile.

- Facebook – In general, Facebook is not a good place to solicit business. It's personal. However, it never hurts to be on the lookout for potential openings. If someone mentions they need help or you can suggest a solution in context, you just might be able to find a contact. But don't be pushy—people aren't expecting a sales pitch on Facebook and will be quickly turned off.

- LinkedIn - Unlike Facebook, LinkedIn is the social network designed for business. This can be a good place to form connections, do some research and keep track of your contacts. It's also a very good place to ask people to introduce you to new contacts. It's easy to be anonymous and impersonal on LinkedIn, so be sure to personalize any interactions you have.

- Craigslist – This one's a crapshoot, but some people have had success. You can post a "job profile," search the job listings or be a little sneaky—browse through the services section and look at websites that could use some help.

Go Meet People

There are lots of ways to actually meet people and develop these relationships, but they all involve getting out of the office. You're going to need to get out there.

Meetups & Events

One of the easiest ways to meet people is at local events. There are many conferences, hangouts and meetups to choose from.

Find (or start) your local WordPress meetup[25] or check out a WordCamp[26]. Or find more general events like CreativeMornings[27]. There are lots of these events around. Check out major sites like Eventbrite[28] or Meetup[29] to see what's going on. You can also ask around for the best local events.

Don't just look for good networking events. Look for events that will help you grow as a freelancer. Maybe it's some kind of professional development or small business class. Or it could just be something that gets your creative juices flowing, whether it's a photo group or an author reading.

When you do make it to these events, take the opportunity to meet people. Sometimes shy people have a hard time, but endure a few awkward moments and introduce yourself. That's why everybody is there. Make some connections.

If you're really nervous, go with a friend. Sometimes it's easier to work the crowd as a duo.

---

25   http://wordpress.meetup.com/
26   http://central.wordcamp.org/
27   http://creativemornings.com/
28   http://www.eventbrite.com/
29   http://www.meetup.com/

Coworking Spaces

For people with a 9-to-5 job many of their relationships come from
their coworkers. Which puts freelancers at a disadvantage. Which is
why you might want to get out of your office and work somewhere
else.

Co-working spaces have sprung up in many cities across the country.
These are shared locations for freelancers to gather and feel like they
have coworkers again. You often need to pay a fee to "rent a desk," but
then you'll have a steady supply of coworkers and potential clients,
collaborators and referrals.

Having a co-working space was a big help for freelance WordPress
developer Bill Erickson:

"That physical space where you could turn around and ask questions
or pull together a team was huge…You need a social community so
you're not on your own".

Lunch or Coffee

Another way to connect with people and go deeper is to meet one-
on-one. Ideally you've already met someone before you ask them to
lunch or coffee. Once you have some form of contact established,
then meeting one-on-one is a great way to develop that freelance
relationship.

Ask lots of questions and find out how you can help them. Figure out
exactly what they do and what type of contact they'll be. Are they a
potential client? A possible freelance collaborator?
Are they someone you could send referrals to?

Remember not to be selfish. Don't monopolize the conversation.

Be sure you pick up the tab and follow up after the meeting. Share a
few connections or resources from your conversation.

Make the meeting have value.

Networking

We've made the case that freelance relationships matter. We've talked about how you can develop those relationships by not being a jerk (among other things) and how you can actually find some freelance friends.

Now you need to do some networking. Some people shudder at the idea of networking. They get images of greasy people working a room with lots of bravado and zealous handshakes. But you don't have to be slimy to network.

Networking is really just about meeting people and finding mutually beneficial connections. **Help other people and they'll help you.** People want to do business with people they know and trust. So build that trust.

Networking is also about more than just meeting people. You need to build those connections. You need to turn them from contacts into clients.

Here's where it helps to remember that it's all about relationships. Build relationships with your contacts. Get to know them and let them get to know you. In time, opportunities will reveal themselves naturally. It's personal relationships that will turn your contacts into contracts.

Here are a few ways you can help the process develop.

Reach Out

First and foremost, you need to take the lead and make the effort. You're the one looking to do more with your contacts. You can't wait around for them to call you, because they won't.

Research

Start with research. In order to make a connection with a contact, you need to know who they are.

- Understand their business. Figure out what they do, who their audience is, how they make their money.

- Check out their website. Notice where it's hosted, who built it and how it's maintained. How's the SEO? What could you improve?

- Google the company. Where do they show up in results. Are they in the news?
- Are they using social media? Follow! Subscribe to blogs, email newsletters and anything else they offer so you can know what they're up to.

Tip: Research a contact's industry as well. A few talking points might help you out in a conversation. Note that the goal isn't to be a know it all— this contact is surely an expert in their own industry, but you want to be informed and engaged. A little knowledge goes a long way.

It's All About Context

You have to offer the right thing at the right time. That's why you did your research. If a contact doesn't need ecommerce, don't talk about it. If a contact doesn't do local, then pitching the benefits of Foursquare is going to be a waste. Make sure what you're talking about is relevant to the contact you're talking to.

That brings us to an obvious conclusion: Every pitch you make is going to be different. Each one should be catered to the specific contact, taking into account their needs, their industry, their approach. You need to customize your pitch so you can maximize its effectiveness. That's why you're taking all this time to get to know contacts—first so you can build a solid relationship in order to make the pitch, but then when you make it you're not shooting in the dark.

You've learned enough about what they need to properly pitch exactly what they need.

Ask, Ask, Ask!

Finally, you need to ask for their business. This is where people fail to convert contacts into clients. They never ask. If you don't ask for their business, you'll never turn a contact into a contract.

Just remember that you've been doing all the groundwork to build a relationship, learn what their company needs and tailor your pitch. Your ask isn't coming out of left field and by now it should be highly targeted. This is no longer a cold call, you're a trusted contact.

Tip: Remember that who you're talking to is important. Your contact may not be the decision maker—but don't pass them up, because they likely have influence with the decision maker. Likewise keep in mind how different pitches may appeal to different departments. The purchasing department might want to save money but the sales staff is only interested in SEO.

Story: Networking

CARRIE DILS, FREELANCE DEVELOPER

What are some of the best practices that keep you successful as a freelancer?

Always be networking. I work alone from home but feel very connected through social media and developer-specific chat groups. I hang out on Twitter a lot, which is basically my go-to spot for "water cooler" conversations when I'm taking a break from work. I've had the opportunity through local WordPress meetups and WordCamps to meet a lot of my social media buddies in real life, which makes the connection even stronger.

Of course, those networks and connections have become part of my referral network, too, so there's a lot of value in cultivating relationships both online and in real life.

In addition to staying socially and professionally connected, setting good work boundaries is important. I've never needed motivation to sit at my desk and work—I love what I do. But I've found it's important to set rules about when I'm not going to work, so I can be present with my family and take care of myself.

New Client Meetings

So you've got a new client meeting to talk about a website project. Awesome. Way to land the meeting.

Now you need to seal the deal. New client meetings are a chance to make a great first impression. This is your chance to stand out from the crowd of freelance developers.

Here are 10 rules to remember for new client meetings:

Rule #1: Do Your Research Before You Meet

This should be obvious, but you'd be surprised at how many freelancers try to wing their new client meeting. That's a good way to fail.

Know what you're getting into ahead of time. Do your research so you can ask intelligent questions.

- Be familiar with their current web presence. Not just their site, but also all their social media outlets.

- Don't stop with their online properties. Check out reviews and what other people are saying. Check out Yelp, Google Maps and do a search for "Client Name Sucks"—you want to know it all.

- Know who their customers are.

- Find out who the important players are in the company—the owner, the president, the founder, etc. Remember to learn the names of the people who don't have fancy titles as well—the person who answers the phone may be just as important to your success at landing the sale.

- Learn their product and understand their mission statement. A new client meeting is a great time to get clarification, but you should make an impression with what you already know.

Rule #2: Treat All People as Clients

You are your brand and people are watching you. Every tiny behavior is noticed. Losing your patience or just acting like a jerk with a random person in the lobby could lose you the job.

You never know who is important and who is not. Don't write someone off just because they're a janitor, secretary or little old lady. Be respectful of everyone.

So be a human: Hold doors open. Smile. Say hello.

Rule #3: Hold New Client Meetings in Person

There's nothing better than sitting across the table from a client. You can look them in the eyes, gauge their reactions and respond on the fly.

It shows you can interact.

It shows you're professional and you value their input.

It shows humanity because you're there. You're real and tangible. That's important because everything you deliver as a developer is an intangible, digital creation.

If an in-person, new client meeting is impossible, at least do it in real time. Set up a video conference or even do the old school phone call. It's not ideal, but at least it's live and you can get immediate reactions.

Doing new client meetings in person instead of just sending a proposal will pay big dividends.

Rule #4: Highlight Existing Positives and How You'll Build On Them

You need to start the conversation with the positives. You want a new client to have a positive initial impression of you, so emphasize the positive.

It doesn't matter how bad their current website is—find something positive to say. Because you don't know the history. The person you're meeting with or the founder's kid might have built their existing site, and by mocking it you've inadvertently offended your not-so-potential client.

Maybe the site is a sore spot and they're embarrassed. Don't make them feel worse.

So find a few things that are positive. Then talk about how you can build on that. At the very worst—they have a site. That's something. They probably get the top search result for their company name and location—even a horrible site can manage that—so there's an SEO foundation you can build on.

Rule #5: Use Resources and Examples

Knock their socks off with charts and graphs. These examples can communicate instantly and that's huge. Create some simple charts to show a few basic things you can improve:

- Website Speed Test[30] – Check out how fast their site is loading.

- Performance Report[31] – Take a look at the site's load time and overall performance.

- Validator [32]– Does the site's code even validate?
- Marketing Grader[33] – Grab all kinds of details, including blogging, social media, SEO, mobile and more.

- Mobile Screenshots – The Chrome browser has an emulator that can show you how a site looks on different devices. Take some screenshots and show how the site looks and how you can make it better.

---

30   http://tools.pingdom.com/fpt

31   http://gtmetrix.com/

32   http://validator.w3.org/

33   https://marketing.grader.com/

Rule #6: Define Metrics of Improvement

Show them where their site is now and how you can make it better. Emphasize things you can track and improve on, like search referrals, traffic, etc. You want to be able to show them success down the road.

This is also a good place to talk about future improvement. The changes you're pitching will help them today, but they'll also help your new client down the road when the site is done and you've moved on to the next project. Don't just talk about now—talk about the future.

Your client wants to hear how this is an investment that will pay off today, tomorrow and into the future. Think bigger than new client meetings.

Rule #7: Talk to the Client Not About the Client

When you're talking to a client about their company and what you can do for them, it can be easy to slip into an abstract way of speaking about the company. That's a good way to depersonalize the conversation and disregard the person sitting across the table.

Instead you should keep it personal. Talk directly to the client. Emphasize how this will impact them, how this will help them do their job. Avoid falling into the abstract and talking about the company. It's about people, not corporations.

Rule #8: Help the Client Dream Outside the Box

A new client meeting is not the time to limit ideas. Help them think big. Don't restrict what they can do during this meeting.

- Ask what they'd love to see on their site.
- Ask what they've seen on other sites that they really like.
- Ask where they want their site to be in two years, five years—even 10 years.

Your goal is to make them think you can do anything. You're an amazing web developer. Don't worry if they bring up something you don't know how to do—that's what sub-contracting is for.

So don't limit this new client meeting to a website they need right now. They could become a long-term client. And you never know where that's going to take you. Maybe today you're building a blog, but who knows what you'll be building tomorrow.

Your client will recognize that this big picture thinking won't happen overnight. It has to be a process. You can scale the dreams back when you're drafting a contract. The dream is where you want to end up, but that means starting with something smaller today.

Rule #9: New Client Meetings Should End With an Action Plan for Both Sides

Before you walk away from the meeting you need to have an action plan in place. Not just for you, but for the client as well. You both need something to do.

If you do not plan an action, no action will happen. If you don't plan for something, you'll get nothing.

Make it a quick and easy so you can get things moving. Tell them you'll send a summary of the meeting within 24 hours and ask them to respond immediately so you know they got it.
Make it clear who is doing what by when.

Rule #10: Always Follow Up With the Client

This is not your action plan from rule #9. This is separate.

Touch base after every new client meeting just to say thanks. Tell them you're looking forward to working with them. That's it.

If a conversation develops, that's great. If not, just say thanks and you look forward to talking later.

And try picking up the phone. Too many people default to email.

The whole point is to reinforce all the positive things from your new client meeting. You're proving that you're someone who follows through. You're polite and great to work with. You're also bringing the meeting back to the forefront—who knows what emergencies they've dealt with since your meeting, pushing the whole thing out of their mind. You're showing the new client that they're a priority to you.

Sometimes a simple follow up can make all the difference.

Rock Your New Client Meeting

Every new client meeting is going to be different, but these general rules should help you make a good impression and land the sale.

Follow Up

Now that you have contacts and you've made the pitch, it's time to follow up.

Under Promise & Over Deliver

If you score the contract, congratulations! Now it's time to deliver. To really impress your new client you need to under promise and over deliver. That strategy will make sure your new client becomes a repeat client, and that your new client talks you up, bringing in more contacts you can convert to more new contracts.

A major way to under promise and over deliver is to do extra work. Maybe your services cover four clearly defined deliverables, but you actually provide five. You don't have to give away the kitchen sink, but just throw in some extra value.

Maybe you do some extra SEO work or deliver a backup copy of your work on CD. Maybe you beat the deadline by a week. Find some way to go above and beyond the call of duty. You'll be glad you did.

Thank You

One of the most important things you can do is say thank you to your new contact turned client. Send them a hand-written note. It will only cost you a few minutes and a stamp, but it will leave a much greater impression.

Tip: If your hand writing is terrible (and let's be honest, that's true for many of us), find another way to make thank you notes work. Maybe it's a pre-printed, semi-generic card for your company and you just write thank you and sign it. That's still personal and will make an impression. The point is to do something.

No Is OK

If you made the pitch and your contact said no, don't fret. It's not the end of the world. You still have them as a contact and you can live to pitch another day. They may have said no for any number of reasons that have nothing to do with you. Maybe they can't afford to do the work right now, maybe they already have someone else in mind or maybe it's just not the right time.

But they're still a contact and a 'no' today doesn't mean 'no' forever. Continue to build a relationship with them and stay in touch. You could still land a contract down the road, so don't give up.

Current Clients

Your best source for new clients? Your current clients. You can maximize your current clients in two ways:

1. Referrals

Most successful freelancers will tell you the bulk of their business comes from referrals. Do good work and stay in touch with your clients (so you remain at the top of their mind) and your chances of scoring referrals goes up astronomically.

You can also actively encourage your current clients to refer new business. An easy way to do this is to offer a reward for a paying referral. Maybe you give a discount on the next job or offer something fun, like a new iPod. You'll make back the cost of the iPod on the new client, and if they stick around long enough you'll make it back ten times over.

2. Repeat Customers

Once a client is your client—don't lose them. You put a lot of work into getting them as a client, so don't let them go. Any client you can keep is one fewer you need to get. Stay engaged with your clients to encourage repeat business. Follow their blogs and updates so you can be proactive and make suggestions to help their business grow.

Tip: Add a specialized footer to each site you build that points back to your site. It's a simple way to let your current clients refer future clients without doing any work.

Professionalism

Be professional. Just because you're a freelancer does not mean it's time for amateur hour.

In fact, because you're a freelancer it's that much more important to communicate a professional and trustworthy image to your clients. They need to know they can rely on you.

Nothing shatters that trust like unprofessionalism: missed deadlines, sloppy communication, lost papers, a TV blaring in the background, etc. Take every opportunity you can to project just how professional you are. Don't give your clients a reason to worry. Give them a reason to trust.

Good Communication Skills

If freelancing is always and forever about people (and it is) then good communication is imperative. Learn how to get better at it.

You can build the greatest websites ever, you can write code that angels envy, but if you can't communicate with others you'll never succeed.

One of our business mentors is fond of saying: "Communication is not the message sent, but the message received."

So you must work continuously, tirelessly on learning how to communicate with the non-geek, non-coders of the world.

Communication with non-techies is truly hard for both sides. It's not that anyone is stupid, it's just that there's an incredible divide to overcome. You speak different languages. And it takes work.

So here are some tips on communicating with the non-geeks of the work world that will benefit your career greatly:

- Be forever patient. Like the long-suffering kind of patient. Stay calm and keep calm, even when you've hit a dead end. Always keep your composure. Never talk down to someone. And remind yourself that we don't talk the same language and this is a communication barrier.

- Translate. After you mention your technical jargon, then say, "This means ..." But the best translations are typically metaphors or analogies. It offers a comparison in terms others can understand.

- See the issue from the other person's point of view, restate what you've heard and ask if your understanding is clear.

- Repeat the *why* until eyes glaze over.

- Explain *how* what you're doing or what you ran into affects the project in terms of time, complexity and budget.

- If development is an expedition, share the hurdles, challenges, dangers of the journey you may run into. Then give options. Don't just give one path of the journey, present different options even if they are all marginal options. And once you've presented the different options, give some input as to what you'd suggest or prefer and most importantly, *why*.

- Seek help and assistance from a translator. Find one of those weird blends of people who can walk and talk in both worlds. They are your ally. Stick close to them. Talk to them often. See how they might translate what you're saying to others.

- Know yourself, know your strengths, know your personality. Understand how you communicate and how it may be different from how other people communicate.

The Technical Details of Communication

In addition to rocking good communication skills that can connect with people, you also need to master the technical skills. Freelancing can often mean working by yourself or remotely, and that can introduce a whole new set of communication problems. Here are some tips to help you master the ins and outs of freelance communication:

- **Shut up and listen:** Sometimes the best thing you can do is be quiet. Let your clients do the talking and you do the listening. As you learn to listen you'll realize that much of your job is figuring out what a client really wants.

- **Learn the tech**: Since you're rarely in the room with the people you work with, it's time to master the various methods of communication that make freelancing so easy: phone, email, text, instant messaging, video conferencing, etc. "We have the technology," says WordPress founder Matt Mullenweg[34]. So use it. Get an account, mess with the settings, make sure you know how it works. Also be aware of the drawbacks. Realize it's hard to understand tone in email.

---

34   http://marketingland.com/why-not-work-from-home-we-have-the-technology-says-wordpress-mullenweg-35814

Know that video conferencing often goes wonky, so call in early to make sure everything works. Learn to use the mute button.

- **Be very available**: Basecamp's Jason Fried[35] emphasizes the importance of overcoming communication barriers: "Since you can't meet face-to-face, you better return phone calls, emails, instant messages, etc. This is basic business stuff, but it's tenfold more important when you're working remotely. … When you're remote, they're going to be more suspicious when phone calls go unreturned or emails keep getting 'lost'. Stay on top of communications and you'll reap the benefits."

- **In the Loop:** Clients have hired you to do a job and you have a responsibility to keep them apprised of how it's going. Different clients will expect different levels of contact. Some will want constant hand holding, while others won't care to talk until the project is complete.

- **Confront problems:** As problems arise, deadlines shift or revisions get out of hand, you must communicate. This is where you need to keep everyone on the same page, make sure the original project scope isn't lost in the shuffle and move the project toward completion. If a client isn't delivering what they need to, you have to let them know. Make sure everyone understands what's happening and what the ramifications are.

- **Build it**: Sometimes the best way to stay connected is to build your own system. That's what Automattic did[36], creating their own P2 WordPress theme and using a password-protected blog structure to encourage conversation among their few hundred employees, most of whom work remotely.

---

35   http://www.inc.com/jason-fried/excerpt-working-with-clients.html

36   http://www.fastcolabs.com/3035463/how-matts-machine-works

That might be overkill for your freelance biz, but it might be a fun way to communicate with your clients.

- **Meetings:** When you have meetings, share the meeting notes with the entire team. Publish them where everyone has access. This not only keeps everyone on the same page, it creates an archive of what decisions you made.

- **Just ask:** We all know what happens when we assume. Your invoice isn't paid and you get mad, assuming your client is stiffing you. Or your project is late and your client gets mad, assuming you're blowing off their project. But in both cases there's probably a simple explanation. Just ask. When everybody knows what's going on, people are less likely to get angry.

Be Organized

You don't really have a choice in this. Freelancing requires organization. Now one person's chaos is another person's anal system, so don't judge. But find an organizational system that works. You need to be able to find those notes, invoices, emails, client files, etc.

Create Systems

"The average worker wastes six weeks a year retrieving misplaced information on office and computer files," says productivity expert Anne McGurty[37]. So whatever system works for you, use it. Don't just dump papers and hope to find them later.

Maybe you have a separate folder in your inbox for each client. Maybe you have a system for tracking your time so you can improve your bids and boost your bottom line.

---

37   http://www.forbes.com/sites/northwesternmutual/2014/08/05/working-from-home-5-tips-for-being-more-productive-remotely/

Maybe you make lists of what you need to accomplish each week and then each day. Maybe you have a system for invoicing and communicating with clients when a project is nearly done.

Whatever you do, you need to keep yourself on track so you get your jobs done. That's the important part. Maybe these systems seem like extra work, but when you're extremely busy and juggling multiple jobs, you'll need some way to keep it all straight. If you already have a system in place, you'll save yourself from the chaos.

Here are some tips to keep your freelance business organized and sane:

- **Organize your notes:** Keep careful notes for each client and each project and keep them organized. You might need a filing cabinet and folders, or a notebook for each client or a folder on your computer—but however you do it, keep it organized. Get a calendar so you can track deadlines and know when you're going to be busy.

- **Keep records:** You'll need to keep careful records so when problems come up you can quickly take care of them. Record every decision, every request and every change. Double check each one and keep the confirmation. You'll save yourself headaches when you can pull out the record and show your client that you were right (in a nice way!).

- **Filer?:** Apparently there are two types of organizing: Filing and piling. If you're a filer, make sure you have enough file drawer space to keep things organized and not be overwhelmed. If you don't have the space for another giant filing cabinet, consider an "archived" filing cabinet in the basement for files you rarely use but still need to keep.

- **Piler?:** If you're a piler, you need to find ways to keep those piles under control. Bins and baskets can help, giving well-labeled, consistent places to pile things. Wall-mounted file holders can also help, allowing you to create piles in more places.

- **Don't stress:** Don't worry if you're a filer or a piler. There are benefits to both[38]: "Working at a prim desk may promote healthy eating, generosity and conventionality, while working at a messy desk promotes creative thinking and stimulates fresh ideas."

- **Close at hand:** Keep important stuff within grasp. If you've got a book you're always referencing or you need paperclips all day long, keep these things close at hand.
  If you're always turning around or reaching for something, it's too far away. Move it closer.

- **Your desk:** Your work desk says a lot about who you are, what you value and how you work. So what does your desk look like? How does it compare to Steve Jobs, Martha Stewart, Albert Einstein or still others? Einstein famously said, "If a cluttered desk is a sign of a cluttered mind, of what, then, is an empty desk a sign?" So while figuring out your desk and workspace is important, don't blindly follow the trends. Find what works for keeping your desk organized (or not organized).

---

38   http://blog.ladiff.com/2013/08/the-piler-vs-the-filer/

Story: Andrew Norcross

ANDREW NORCROSS, FREELANCE DEVELOPER, REAKTIV
STUDIOS

What was your first breakthrough in business that made you successful and how did it come about?

I don't think there was one big "breakthrough" event, but rather a series of small wins and lessons.

I was fortunate to get involved at a time when WordPress was growing, but wasn't the crowded space it is today. I put in a lot of time and effort and made a lot of mistakes, but was lucky that I could recover from them.

It also helped that due to some things in my personal life, I had begun freelancing without much (none, really), of a safety net so I had extra motivation to make it work.

Can you share a few of those mistakes and what you learned?

Oh wow, there are so many it's not even funny.

But a few core ones that took more than a few times to grasp:

- Learning client red flags.
- Listening to my gut when something didn't seem right.
- Only promising what I can actually deliver.
- When I mess something up, owning it 100%.

You've worked full-time jobs as well as running your own business, Reaktiv Studios. What keeps bringing you back to running your own business?

I worked for two companies for a total of 18 months in the middle of my now 8-year career. It was a combination of being exhausted running my company solo, wanting to purchase a home and getting married, which brought two more kids to the family. So the insurance, steady pay, etc., was nice. It also gave me a chance to work on some cool projects that I wouldn't have gotten as a freelancer.

But ultimately I'm just not that good at working for other people, as I've never done well with authority. So when I re-launched Reaktiv full time, my wife took on the management side of the business while I focused on the development side. It's worked out amazingly well.

What's your best advice for working with clients?

First off, do the work.

It seems odd to say, but so many issues are avoided by just delivering on your promises.

From there, it's a matter of communication. Let them know what's happening. Get them involved when they need to be (and push them out when they don't). And most importantly, be the professional.

Appearance

People like to joke about freelancers working in their pajamas, and if that works for you, great. But very few freelancers are going to get the gig showing up for a client meeting like that. You have to be professional.

Here are some tips for looking and feeling professional and productive:

- **Suit up:** We like to pretend it's not true, but image matters. Go casual at home or the office if you like, but when you're meeting with clients or networking, image really does matter. If you want people to think you're professional, dress like a professional.

- **Dress for success:** "There is a real psychological benefit to dressing for your job even when you're at home." So says *Inc Magazine*[39]. As does All in One SEO Pack developer Michael Torbert[40]: "Dressing professionally gives other people the impression that you're a professional, and it makes you feel like one". Of course others would argue the psychological benefits of being comfortable. Like many of these tips, your mileage may vary. Some people find that the right clothes help them shift into a professional mindset. They work better in khakis. Other people could care less and being comfortable in their pajamas makes them more efficient. Figure out what works for you.

- **Remember the Skype call:** If you do opt to dress down at home, just remember to step it up when you're doing video conference calls. You may wear pajamas every day, but your clients don't need to know that.

- **Shoes:** If you do need help shifting into that professional mode, remember the details. Sometimes shoes can make all the difference. Not wearing shoes is lounging around on the couch with your feet up. Wearing shoes is going out, ready for serious business.

---

39   http://www.inc.com/jayson-demers/10-habits-to-work-from-home-effectively.html?cid=sf01001

40   http://startupsofa.com/9-ways-to-get-serious-about-your-work/

- **Exercise your clothes:** For Team Casual, a very real problem is your professional clothes may never get used. If you only pull them out once a year, you might find they've literally collected dust. Remember that when you have an in-person meeting— and preferably not an hour before the meeting when there's nothing you can do about the dust crease in your dress pants. Bust out those dress clothes once in a while and give them some exercise. Overdress for a networking meeting or a date with your significant other. Even if you don't like dressing up, you may find you like it better when it's not a workplace requirement.

Timing

Timing matters for professional freelancers. You've got to put in the hours, you've got to sync schedules with clients in different time zones and you absolutely must hit those deadlines. You've also got find a routine that works for you.

A few tips to keep your freelance business on time:

- **Set your hours:** Yes, you can work whenever you want. But that's not always helpful or practical. For the sake of the people you work with, you might need to set specific hours. If you need to be available or if you want people to actually pick up the phone when you call, you might need to have 9-to-5 hours.

- **In the zone:** When you set your hours, work when you work best. If you're a morning person, schedule your prime hours in the morning. Take advantage of your sweet spot.

- **Routine:** Rather than being in a rut, a routine is a good way to be more productive. While you might chafe at starting work at the same time every morning, that routine is good for productivity. It also means you're more likely to be done at the same time every evening. Working at home shouldn't have to mean burning the midnight oil on a regular basis.

- **Flexibility:** But for all this talk of set hours and routines, flexibility is perhaps one of the greatest reasons to freelance. Being able to run errands, mow the lawn before it rains or attend school field trips with your kids is pretty great. Just recognize that it works both ways. Sacrificing a morning to run errands means working in the evening to make up for it. Running off to the beach on Monday means you'll be putting in time on Saturday. Flexibility is great, just be sure you find the balance.

- **Be focused:** Sometimes freelancing can be a bit scattered. You don't have a boss breathing down your neck or a project manager telling you what's next. You need to be your own project manager. So each day create a task list of what you need to get done that day. Set out specific tasks for each day. This will help you stay on track and give you a target to know you're getting done what you need to.

- **Mini-routine:** A daily routine is helpful, but so is creating smaller routines throughout your day. Adding structure to your day can make you more productive. The pomodoro technique[41] is one way to structure your day. It involves using a timer and focusing on specific tasks for 25 minutes and then taking 5 minute breaks. It can be a good way to power through difficult (or dreaded) tasks and then reward yourself with a limited break (the timer keeps a quick Facebook check-in from turning into 20 minutes).

- **Track hours:** Even if you don't bill hourly, track your hours. It's essential to know how much time you need to finish a job so you can know if you're charging enough. It's also helpful to see how productive you're being.

- **Break time:** Yes, you should take breaks. For sanity, health and productivity, it's important to tear yourself away from work.

---

41   http://en.wikipedia.org/wiki/Pomodoro_Technique

Go to the kitchen for a glass of water and a quick snack. Take a walk around the block. Change that load of laundry. On-site office workers get breaks, and so should you. Just make sure break time doesn't mean the latest episode of *The Walking Dead*.

- **Reward yourself:** In addition to taking breaks, you should also reward yourself. Set goals for finishing a project or putting in so many hours, then reward yourself. Maybe it's that episode of The Walking Dead or maybe it's quitting early. Obviously you can't do this every day, but if you're nearing the end of a project and need that extra push, a little reward can help. You can also set smaller rewards like a piece of candy or a few minutes of YouTube. Figure out what motivates you. Most freelancers are pretty self-motivated, but sometimes you need that extra push.

- **Don't quit when it's hard:** All freelancers face days when everything is hard and you just want to quit. Don't. Stick with it. It's a dangerous precedent to slack off work every time something gets hard. Take a five-minute break. Work on a different project. Do some mindless busy work like cleaning your office. Just keep working. Freelancing requires determination.

- **Time zones:** Freelancing often means dealing with the dreaded time zone. You may be working with clients on the other side of the country or even the planet. The biggest thing you can do to overcome time zones is to communicate clearly about them. Always include the time zone when talking schedules. It can often help to convert the time zone for the person you're talking to. Remember to be flexible. You might need to shift your schedule so you can be in the office when the people you're working with are.

- **Off schedule:** Sometimes those time zones can be an advantage. While it's helpful to work at the same time as your clients, sometimes it's better to do your serious work when no one else is working. You can do your heads-down work without interruption.

- **No eight-hour days:** It can be a rough transition from working eight hours a day in an office to freelancing. Especially when you realize that billing eight hours a day often requires working 10- or 12-hour days. There's all this extra work that's not billable—checking email, phone calls, breaks, networking, research, invoicing, etc. You might need to revise your expectations. Rather than feel guilty, remember what it was like in the office—breaks, conversations with coworkers, distractions, etc. Plan for that in your schedule.

- **Cushion:** Work more so you can work less. The flexibility of freelancing is great, but in order to truly take advantage of it you need to work extra so you have a cushion for the unexpected. If you rigidly work 8 hours every day, then on Friday afternoon you still have to finish your 8 hours before you can call it a weekend. But if every day you worked even half an hour extra, by Friday you'd be able to quit two hours early. **It's easy to take time off, but it's harder to put it in.** So work extra when you can. Then take off when you need to.

- **Punctuality matters:** Be early for meetings and nail your deadlines. The world is moving faster all the time and nobody has time for a freelancer who shows up late or can't meet a deadline. If you want to impress a client and stand out, always finish a project early. That'll turn some heads.

Story: Be Productive

BRIAN CASEL, FREELANCE DESIGNER

How do you choose what to work on?

In years past, every day I would work on something new based on a whim. Today I want to work on this project or today I feel like coding so I'll open up Coda, or today I want to design so I'll open up Photoshop.

But I've learned in the past year that it's **important to be strategic**, to look at the big picture. What are the big projects you want to do? Look at a year, then a month, then a week. Then decide what's on the agenda for today. Really, there should be one big thing to get done. There's always more stuff to do, but you at least want to accomplish one big thing every day. Being goal oriented and planning ahead, that really helps.

One day a month, usually during the beginning of the month, I'll spend a whole day thinking about what should I get done this month, what should I be working on? When you dedicate that time to being strategic, rather than "I'm in the mood to design something," or "This client's deadline is looming, I need to work on this, it's seemingly urgent." I think it's important to be strategic about what you work on. **Work on things that make you uncomfortable.** Be honest with yourself about areas of the business where you're weak.

Here's a good example: I completely redesigned my marketing site six months ago because we weren't selling as quickly as I wanted. I thought the problem was the design, but really I wanted to redesign the site and I was good at it.

But it didn't help sales. What helped sales was improving our marketing funnel. That's something I didn't know much about at the time. So I put it off. When I finally got into it and decided I'd focus on improving our sales and marketing funnel, that's when we saw a noticeable improvement in sales. All it took was research, learning and trying a few new things I hadn't worked on before.

Office Space

Your work environment has a tremendous impact on how well you do your work. This is a serious job so you need a serious work space. You can't just set up an office in the living room or throw open your laptop wherever you are and call it an office. You need a space where you can buckle down and do your work. You need somewhere where you can work undisturbed, somewhere where you can take phone calls and not have children screaming or dogs barking.

Getting out and working in a coffee shop can be great, but it's hard to make that your permanent space. You can always rent an office or consider a co-working location.

Here are some tips for making your work space professional and productive:

- **Dedicated space:** You need a designated workspace that isn't used for anything else. You don't want to bounce around from the kitchen to the den. It doesn't have to be an entire room, but it should be space that's set aside for work. This can help you shift into the work mentality.

- **Flexible space:** That's not to say you can't work somewhere else. Sometimes sitting down at the kitchen table instead of your desk can get you out of a rut. Sometimes spreading out on the floor is just what you need.

Having a desk is good, but don't feel stuck there.

- **Location, location, location**: Pick a home office location that's going to work for you. High traffic areas can be distracting. If your office is off a family room, will the TV be too much of a temptation? Especially when someone is watching it?

- **Natural light:** Windows can make a big difference in your working atmosphere. Find a space with plenty of natural light.

- **Too hot? Too cold?:** Pay attention to the temperature when you pick an office location. You don't want to be working in your skivvies in the summer because the AC can't cool the attic enough.

- **Shut the door:** A lot of people need to close the door on distractions. If that's you, it helps to have a door. If you've got a corner of the dining room or an extra space that doesn't have a door, that can be a problem. Home offices are often after thoughts, and that means odd spaces and often no door. From people barging in to excess noise, no door means more distractions.

- **Get some color:** "Forget 'office beige,'" says HGTV[42]. "You need a color that gets your work motor humming." Paint your office walls a color that works. For some people that's something bold and bright, others want something more subtle and soothing. Figure out what works for you and spice up your space.

---

42   http://www.hgtv.com/design/rooms/other-rooms/1/10-tips-for-designing-your-home-office

- **Comfy is good:** Comfy space is "the overlooked perk of the home office," according to Linda Varone[43], author of *The Smarter Home Office*. "If you've got room for it, it is one of the best things you can do for yourself." A comfy couch is a good place to relax with a stack of reading or do some doodling on a clipboard. It's a way to keep working without always being chained to your desk.

- **Change it up:** "When things don't get changed around they become somewhat like wall paper," says Linda Varone. Those motivational posters become invisible and aren't so motivating. Your desk toys get pushed under stacks of paper and forgotten. Change your decorations, move things around, keep your office feeling fresh.

- **Be creative:** Make your home office inspiring and energizing. Figure out what makes you creative and put that stuff in your space. Maybe it's cool posters or funky artwork. Maybe it's desk toys or a whiteboard. Make it your own.

- **Put your walls to work:** Get the most out of your walls by making them double as whiteboards. IdeaPaint[44] can turn any wall into a whiteboard.

- **Minimize distractions:** Some people need to go minimal and have nothing on their desk. That might be too far, but try to minimize the distractions. You don't want a pile of laundry making you feel guilty. You also don't want a stack of bills pulling you away from a deadline.

- **Experiment:** Don't rush out and spend loads of money on new furniture all at once. Try things out and see what works.

---

43   http://www.fastcompany.com/3023303/work-smart/10-quick-tips-to-bring-your-home-office-to-another-level

44   http://www.ideapaint.com/

Rearrange your office a few times. Is it better to face the window? Do you get a glare on your screen? Is that desk working or do you need something bigger/smaller/shorter?

- **Tax breaks:** There is a home office deduction and all the stuff you buy for your office is a business expense. Keep receipts and write it off. Talk to a tax professional to learn more about the home office deduction.

Making your office space work—so you can work—is a big step toward professionalism.

Boundaries & Expectations

Part of being taken seriously as a freelancer is setting real boundaries and expectations, both in your professional and your personal life.

Let your clients know when you're working and when you're not. It's easy for the freelance world to be all-consuming, but part of being professional is taking care of yourself (more on that later). You need some time off to rest and recuperate, and that will only happen if you set boundaries with your clients. **Let them know what to expect and they'll respect you for it.**

You also need to set boundaries and expectations for your family and friends if you're going to be professional. If you're working at home it can be easy for your family to think you are home. Suddenly they're marching in with homework questions and just shooting the breeze. Let your family know that when the door is closed you're working and not to be disturbed. Or set specific hours for yourself. It can be hard to turn the family away, but you also need to get work done.

The flip side is that you can be more available. Just be sure your family understands how the give and take works. If you take the afternoon off to watch your daughter's softball game and need to work that evening, make sure she understands.

It's all a balancing act, but when everyone knows what to expect, it goes a lot smoother. Let's go over a few tips for finding that balance with a family at home:

- **Work zone:** Set clear expectations and boundaries with your family when you work from home. Everyone in the house needs to understand what it means when you're at work. Let everyone know when it's OK to interrupt and when it's not.

- **Stoplight:** Here's an idea from John Meyer[45], CEO of Arise Virtual Solutions, a work-at-home call center company: Hang colored construction paper on your office door.
"Tape the red light up when you cannot be disturbed and the green light when it's OK to come in. Yellow light means to check first," he says. "Kids, no matter what age, understand the message and enjoy playing along."

- **Heads up:** Make those boundaries easier by letting your family know when you've got a call and can't be disturbed. Before your call, check in to see if anyone needs anything from you before you can't be disturbed. It's a good way to head off any issues and remind those forgetful kids that you'll be busy.

- **Go away:** Instead of kids you may be dealing with friends or family dropping in to say hello. It's not breaking up fights, but it can be just as disruptive to your day. Here's where you're going to need to set firm boundaries and decide how flexible you can be and still be productive. If it's once in a great while, don't be so hard-nosed and take a break to chat it up with your friend. But if it's your mom stopping in every other day to shoot the breeze, put your foot down.

---

45   http://www.inc.com/christina-desmarais/get-more-done-18-tips-for-telecommuters.html

- **Work with it:** Setting boundaries and shutting the door on your kids isn't always possible. Some work-at-home parents need to keep a sharp eye on young kids and still get work done. Sometimes that means sitting at the kitchen table with the laptop so you can watch the kids play. Sometimes that means putting a baby gate across the door and a pile of toys in a corner (oddly, that works for the puppy too). Maybe you have a coloring table in your office (and upgrade to Legos when they get older). Realize that you're not going to be as efficient and it's not an ideal set up, but sometimes you have to get work done and take care of your kids at the same time.

- **Give up:** Geof Hilman[46], a father of three, says: "Just embrace it— kid interruptions are my water cooler time."

- **Phone rules:** If you have a dedicated business line then you probably don't need many phone rules for the rest of the family, though you should be sure no one answers the phone in your office. But if you're sharing your business line with your house line, you should have clear rules about answering the phone. Either teach your kids how to politely answer the phone or ask them not to answer it.

- **Hands off:** Your computer is a tool for work. It's not a toy for the rest of the family. Don't let anyone else use it, unless you're willing to risk sticky spills on the keyboard and bizarre viruses. Decide what boundaries you're comfortable with, but protect your computer.

---

46   http://www.inc.com/francesca-fenzi/how-to-set-work-boundaries-at-home.html

Client Conflicts

Client conflicts and project problems are never expected or welcomed circumstances in freelancing. Who wants to deal with an unhappy client or project gone bad? You want to avoid these situations like the Ebola virus. It's unhealthy for you, as well as the people around you. Unfortunately we're all going to be exposed to some of these problems in our freelancing journey, but the good news is that we can prevent a majority of them from happening.

How to Prevent Client Conflicts

The number one reason client conflicts happen is because of a lack of clear communication. Misunderstandings happen. It's the nature of the business. Yet you can eliminate so many problems by making sure you give as much information to your client as possible. Even to the point it seems extraneous. There are specific details and elements of every project that you should be clear about:

- **Scope of project:** What is included with your project fee and what isn't? List every detail out so there is no question about what you are providing and what you aren't! This should always be your priority in any proposal you send out.

- **Timeframes:** Provide your client with milestones or dates for when they can expect your work to be done. Be realistic and don't underestimate this. Remember it's better to under-promise and over deliver than over promising and not delivering.

- **Client Expectations:** Clients expect you to do your work and deliver on time and on budget, but you should also set defined expectations for what your client needs to do as well. Let them know that if they don't follow through with their expectations that it can delay the work or increase the cost of the project.

- **Payment Schedule and Terms:** If you want to be successful as a freelancer, you're going to have to get great at asking for money and business terms that benefit your business. Conflicts can arise when you don't let clients know when you want to be paid and how you provide your services. Be upfront on these items.

- **Project Conflicts:** It seems funny to add this to the list, but sometimes you need to include a process in your contracts when client conflict happens. Do you want to have a three-step process for resolving disputes? Will you need to bring in legal counsel for instances you or the client threatens to sue? Thinking through and preparing for the bad circumstances is always beneficial should it happen to you.

Providing detailed information to your clients regarding the project is always going to help you—and them—in the long run.

Tips for When Client Conflicts Arise

When it comes to conflicts, we typically have two responses—fight or flight. For some people, it's easy to become extremely defensive and want to meet the conflict head on, but this will only make matters worse. Other people prefer to run and hide under a rock, hoping the troubles will pass by. This will also make matters worse. So what do you do?

1. Keep Calm and Carry On

Seriously. While those memes have been used ad nauseam, there really is no substitute for keeping calm in problematic situations. Take a deep breath and then wait to respond.

2. Assess the Problem

Look at the entire situation from every angle. Put yourself in your client's shoes to see what they might be dealing with. Assess whether you've covered all your bases or if you've dropped the ball. Be honest and be fair.

3. Respond Professionally

Whatever the situation, it is always best to respond as professionally as possible. Don't take any attacks personally and remember this is a business transaction. Be polite and be careful what you say. You can easily turn a fiasco into a triumph by being professional.

4. Take a Clear and Committed Course of Action

It is now likely up to you to determine what happens next. Can you resolve the conflict and make the client happy? Will you need to fire the client and refund their money? Whatever your decision, you need to be upfront and clear with the client. You then need to follow through and not waiver.

5. Move On

Once you've made your decision, whatever that might be, you need to put it behind you and not dwell on it. This is solely for your benefit.

There is one last but very important piece of advice that can make a tremendous difference between a happy ending or a horrible nightmare:

Be honest! Own your mistakes and don't make excuses or pass blame. If you do, you'll find a lot more forgiveness and often even more business. Sometimes all our clients want are real, honest answers.

If you practice these tips, client conflicts and project problems will be greatly minimized. Even if you do happen to get into a bad situation, you can be fully prepared to handle it like a professional freelancer should.

Take Care of Yourself

It's easy as a freelancer to throw yourself into your work. The problem is that you don't realize how you're throwing yourself away.

You need to take care of yourself.

And that doesn't mean you go full throttle until your breaking point (or past it) and then take a vacation. Your career isn't a sprint, it's a marathon. So pace yourself.

In this chapter we'll talk about a number of ways to take care of yourself, including staying healthy, juggling the personal and professional, the importance of learning and the value you can find in passing on what you learn to others.

Take a Break

We all need to rest and recharge.

There will always be deadlines, milestones and a feature list to chase.

Figure out what is the key to how you best rest and recharge. Then schedule it out.

Give people plenty of notice and do something that almost forces you to actually take the time off (buying plane tickets, etc.). If you don't truly power down you're a great candidate for burnout. And that's no good for anyone.

And it's ultimately your responsibility to watch the gauges of your energy, focus and patience. When you start to go low on all of those, you're going to start to become hard to work with and short tempered.

It's so important to know yourself and then take an appropriate amount of downtime.

It's amazing how much better you'll be after some time off. And downtime means powering off as much as possible. Maybe you leave your phone on but you're not checking email or on chat.

When you take time to rest and recharge, when you come back you'll be more creative. You'll be more passionate. You'll be more focused. You'll be more open and eager to explore options. And it's likely during your downtime, the solution to a nagging problem has bubbled up. Those are all the great byproducts of rest.

- **Read a book:** About something completely unrelated to programming.

- **Take a cooking class:** It's working with your hands and a lot of fun when you can eat your end result.

- **Start learning a new language:** Not PHP or Ruby, but Spanish or Chinese.

- **Experience nature:** Go on a hike, or a rafting trip, or go snow skiing. Something in the outdoors.

Stay Healthy

Going freelance can mean working at home, never leaving the office and turning into a sedentary sloth. That's bad. **Make healthy choices about your career.** Don't slip into bad habits just because you're at home and no one can judge your chocolate binge.

We've got some health tips to make your home office and your freelance career good for you.

- **Ergonomics**: Don't forget to consider ergonomics. If you're working at a computer all day, you need to have the right equipment so you're not hurting yourself. Make sure your monitor is at the right height and distance. Get a keyboard tray. Consider a hardcore ergonomic keyboard (developer Divya Manian[47] recommends the Kinesis Advantage[48]; the Kinesis Freestyle[49] with optional tenting add-on is pretty good too). An ergonomic mouse is also a good investment (the Evoluent[50] vertical mouse looks funky but has a natural feel). Carpal tunnel or "wrist overuse syndrome" (yes, that's an actual diagnosis), are serious business.

- **Let there be light:** Don't strain your eyes. Get some lamps and brighten up the place. You may be awash in daylight in the summer, but you don't want your workspace feeling dismal at night or all winter long.

- **Sit on it:** Get a good office chair. It's one of the best investments you can make. Don't get a cheap chair or try to get away with a spare kitchen chair. Buy a quality, comfy office chair. Your back (and your butt) will thank you.

---

47   http://divya.manian.usesthis.com/

48   http://www.kinesis-ergo.com/shop/advantage-for-pc-mac/

49   http://www.kinesis-ergo.com/shop/freestyle2-blue-mac/

50   http://evoluent.com/

And definitely experiment to find the best chair. Blogger Jason Kottke had back trouble that he traced to the wheels on his desk chair. "I switched from a wheeled chair to a plain old chair and voila, no more back issues," Kottke says[51].

- **Get up:** But once you get that good chair, don't sit in it all day. Sitting is bad for you[52]. Find ways to get off your butt and get moving. Take breaks to stretch, go for quick walks or consider a standing desk.

- **Liven it up:** All kinds of studies have shown the health benefits of houseplants (here's one where they made a bunch of old people less crabby[53]). Get some plants in your workspace. Just remember to actually care for them. A dead plant in the corner is kind of demotivating.

- **Beware of handy food:** One of the potential downsides of working at home is a fully-stocked fridge just steps away. A sedentary job paired with all-day snacking is not good for your waistline. Do yourself a favor and stock some healthy snacks— yogurt, cheese sticks, nuts, fruit, etc.

- **Leftovers:** Another cost-saving advantage to working at home is you can be sure to finish off those leftovers.

- **Get exercise:** Quick access to the fridge and a sedentary job mean that proper exercise is even more important. Make your flexible schedule work for you—exercise first thing in the morning and combine your morning shower and post-run shower. Why waste time showering twice a day?

---

51   http://jason.kottke.usesthis.com/

52   http://www.inc.com/articles/0502/action-tips-for-healthy-employees.
html

53   http://www.rodalenews.com/plants-and-happiness

- **Exercise at home:** Heading to the gym can be yet another way to get some human interaction outside the office. But if you're not struggling with that, exercising at home will save you time. Consider a stationary bike (or bike stand) or take up running in your neighborhood. The 20 minutes driving to and from the gym is time you don't need to give up.

- **Save your eyes:** Staring at a screen all day is bad for your eyes, so give them a break. Developer Jennifer Wong[54] recommends a couple "weird apps": 20 Cubed[55] is a Chrome extension that reminds you to look away from your computer every 20 minutes, and f.lux[56] dims or brightens your screen based on the time of day.

54   http://jennifer.wong.usesthis.com/

55   http://lifehacker.com/5872378/20-cubed-for-chrome-reminds-you-to-rest-your-eyes-and-take-a-break

56   https://justgetflux.com/

Story: Keep Growing

BILL ERICKSON, FREELANCE DEVELOPER

What keeps you successful as a WordPress freelancer?

Success from a business perspective is doing high quality work and building your client list. Word of mouth is the primary source—recommendations from past clients. I could take down my website right now and still have work coming in—that's how important word of mouth is.

As far as success from a personal perspective, if you keep doing the same thing you're going to slowly get left behind. The market keeps moving and you need to move with it. So you need to interact with other developers and see what they're doing so you can keep growing.

That's a lot more difficult as a successful developer than when you're just coming up. You're too busy with all your projects to try out the latest things. It's kind of a problem of success, I guess. But when you've found something that works, it's hard to take time away to learn something new, especially when you don't know if it's going to be successful.

Right now I'm trying to carve out time to test new technology and expand my skill set, even though I'm fully booked. Especially when you've already given 120% to clients, that research is the easiest thing to cut. It's like the cobbler's shoes—it takes forever for web developers to do their own sites.

Human Interaction

One of the hazards of freelancing is loneliness. We've already talked about the importance of building freelance relationships and how getting out of the office is a good way to find clients. But loneliness still lurks when you're trapped in the office all day. When that happens, you need to find ways to get human interaction, hopefully while still getting your work done.

Here are some tips to get you away from the computer and seeing real live people:

- **Face to face:** One of the most common complaints from people who work from home is the lack of real world interaction. Seeing nothing but your cats all day can drive you crazy. So be sure to get out and meet real people in the flesh. Try to get out of the house at least once a week.

- **Any human:** And that personal interaction doesn't have to be business related. Basecamp's David Heinemeier Hansson[57] says, "One of the key insights we've gained through many years of remote work is that human interaction does not have to come from either coworkers or others in your industry. Sometimes, even more satisfying interaction comes from spending time with your spouse, your children, your family, your friends, your neighbors: people who can all be thousands of miles away from your office, but right next to you."

- **Run errands:** Even if you don't have a business reason to leave the house, go run some errands. Pick up some milk. Sometimes that 15-minute trip is enough of a change of pace.

- **Change of scenery:** Something that can help with the lack of human interaction is a change of scenery.

---

57   https://signalvnoise.com/posts/3658

Go work at a coffee shop, sure, but sometimes it's as simple as moving to the kitchen or the deck.

- **Know thyself:** Once again it's important to know yourself. How much human interaction do you need? For some introverts working in an office all day is exhausting. They come home ready to curl up and ignore the world. But working from home all day with no interaction might mean that same introvert is ready to get out and see people at the end of the day. Know what you need and how it might change if you work from home.

- **Get together:** Local meetups are a great way to get that personal interaction and do some networking. There are lots of events you can check out, so ask around, do some searching and get together.

- **Let's eat:** Lunch meetings are an ideal way to get out of the office and interact with people. Everybody needs to eat, so you might as well get some face time and build your network while you're at it.

- **Support local:** Find a coffee shop near your house that can be your satellite office. Support your local businesses so they don't disappear. Consider the cost of a cup of coffee (or your preferred beverage) to be your rent for sitting at a table for an hour (and if you're going to be there all day, buy more than a cup of coffee).

- **Small talk:** The business world is very anti-meetings these days. People want to get back to work and get stuff done, and meetings tend to suck the life out of productivity. That can be difficult when you're working from home and your only interaction is those meetings. Push for those meetings to happen anyway and allow some time for small talk. Keep your meetings productive, but it's also productive for you to get some interaction with your team. Just because it's a conference call doesn't mean you have to be all business all the time.

- **Fake it:** Sometimes you just can't get human interaction when you work from home. You've got to buckle down and work. You can try faking it with TV, music or other background noise. You need to find something that's not distracting. Some people can't work with talk radio on. Other people can't not watch TV. But the right background noise, whether it's classical music or soap operas, can help you focus and be more productive.

Always Be Learning
If you're not learning, you're dying.

So always find something new to learn—even if that's another programming language, new framework, whatever. But never be satisfied with the knowledge you have today.

The best companies hire learners. The best managers and team leads want learners on their teams.

Being a learner means you're not content to stay where you are for the rest of your life. You know you're an unfinished product and you have much more to learn in life.

Never forget: 16-year-old geniuses are plugging away in their parent's basement who are going to rock your world. They're eager to learn. Are you?

Read Stuff
The best learners read. And they read voraciously.

You should always have a new book on your desk or in your library or on your phone. You should be reading things that:

- Stretch you
- Expand your knowledge

- Give you a broader perspective on the world
- Help you improve as a person

Invest in Your Learning

Also, learn and grow on your own time and dime.

If you're not freelancing yet and you're still on the company payroll, *never* rely solely on your boss or organization to invest in your skills. **Invest in yourself.** Make the time. Write the check. Because at the end of the day, you take those skills with you.

And when you're freelancing, *always* invest in yourself. Put learning and growth in the budget and on the calendar.

Story: Work on Your Own Stuff
BRIAN CASEL, WEB DESIGNER

Make an effort to break off a chunk of your time—maybe 20%—to work on your own projects. Don't be completely involved in just client work. You want to be doing stuff for yourself as well. That's how you get better, that's how you push your own creative style further.

Maybe that's redesigning your own site. I do that every six months just because I want to. That's a great way to flex the creative muscles. Just because the time is not billable doesn't mean you shouldn't be using the time to be creative.

Never stop learning and never stop trying new things. I think it's really important to work on your own projects. Even if it's something that will never see the light of day, just work on something for yourself and balance that with the stuff you do for clients.

Check Arrogance at the Door

The best coders don't have to announce their greatness. They let their code speak for itself.

The best coders I've known have quiet confidence and check their ego at the door for the greater good. These are the developers people yearn to work with. Show up. Do the work. Ship. And the glory will come.

If you have an insatiable desire to tell the world all the awesomeness about yourself, all the time, then something's a little off, honestly.

In fact, you probably have a confidence problem.

Most people in life don't want to work with arrogant people.

Words are vapor. When you add a thick cologne of arrogance to it, it becomes hot air.

And you can achieve so much more in your work and your career with action than mere words. Action breeds a quiet confidence because we all know you show up, do the work and deliver. The fewer words required the better.

So learn quiet confidence and humility through action.

You'll be more popular and people will love you and your work even more.

And then when you hit that milestone and deliver on your project, they're going to make a really big deal out of you and your work because you didn't do it already.

Juggling Professional & Personal

Running your own business can be all-consuming. While we all want to find freelance success, it's also important to maintain a personal life.

Let's talk tips for juggling the professional and the personal:

- **In the office:** A good way to separate your work life and your home life when you work from home is to keep work in the office. Take breaks outside your office, limit your work to the office. Don't spill out to the kitchen table. You'll have to figure out what works best for you, but this can be a good way to keep yourself focused on work.

- **After hours:** Another good way to separate work and home life is to not work after hours. Put in your daily hours and be done. Close up shop. Shut down the computer. Stop checking messages on your phone. You can always be flexible when you need to be, but not every work email is an emergency.

- **Working too much:** A lot of managers bristle at the idea of working at home because they think there's going to be too much sleeping in and watching TV and not enough working. But often the opposite is true: people working from home work too much. They love their job, their job is at home, and so it's hard to enforce boundaries. This is a big thing for freelancers to work against.

- **Overworked:** "One way to help set a healthy boundary is to encourage employees to think in terms of a 'a good day's work,'" says Basecamp's Jason Fried[58]. "Look at your progress at the end of the day and ask yourself: "Have I done a good day's work?"

58　　　　http://www.inc.com/jason-fried/excerpt-true-challenge-of-remote-workers

- **Alignment:** Some people talk about finding balance between work and home, and how hard that is when you do both in the same place. But Chris Lema[59] prefers alignment. Forget the tug-of-war between work life and home life. You've only got one life. So find alignment.

Pass It On

As you become a successful freelancer, you have a responsibility to pass what you know on to someone else a couple of steps behind you. You need to share your lesson and your journey with Past You. Seek to be a mentor, teacher, trainer, helper to people you interact with and in your sphere of influence.

Giving back to someone else, for their ultimate benefit and not yours is actually one of the most rewarding things you can do in your career.

Multiplying ourselves, and giving ourselves and our experiences and expertise away, for someone else's benefit, is the upper echelons of finding purpose and meaning.

It's likely you were helped at some point in your life by others passing down their knowledge and wisdom to you. We should pledge to do the same for others. Pass it on by paying it forward. This is about seeking a lasting legacy in and through your work by investing in others.

And the best way to do that is to be a mentor and coach or simply a friendly ear to those seeking the same freelance success you are.

In this way, we find deeper and richer purpose by multiplying our lives and our impact well into the next generation and beyond.

---

59   http://chrislema.com/work-life-balance-goal/

If you feel like you're not quite an expert yet, don't let that be an excuse. You just need to be two to three steps ahead of someone else who wants to get to where you are now. It's simply showing them the way, pointing out those two to three steps they need to take from here to there.

It's like an indoor climbing wall with the brightly colored hand and foot holds. You are higher on the wall than the person seeking the same goals as you. They are headed up the wall just like you in the same direction. You are simply ahead of them. As you look down the wall, you simply point to the next hold you took when you were there. And yes, it's really that simple. Anyone can be a coach and a mentor with that attitude.

So here are some tips for how to give yourself away to others and in the process multiply yourself in their lives:

Be an Unselfish Giver

You must want their ultimate best, with no price tag attached. It means giving so they gain without thought or worry about your own. People quickly recognize the difference between selfish and unselfish giving.

Be Friendly

Always be open to meeting new friends, and specifically good people who have great potential. Some people give off the rockstar vibe so they aren't approachable. Be the opposite. Seek to know who people are and how you can help them. Work to be known as a nice and friendly person because isn't that the kind of person you want to work with?

Be Open

There's plenty of work out there and you don't need to guard your territory. Be open with others, even if they might be your competition. Develop a relationship and help one another out. You'll likely gain more from helping one another than you will from shutting each other out in fierce competition.

Be Available

Have coffee or lunch with people as often as you can. It may be a sacrifice in time and energy, but it will pay dividends in relationships and connections. Open up your calendar to people.

Be Helpful

Help people out. Point to that next handhold on the climbing wall, whether it's making an introduction or giving some advice.

Do these things, or rather *be* these things, and people will seek you out.

Story: Share What You Know

CORY MILLER, FOUNDER, ITHEMES

After I left college and started my first professional gig, a friend of mine who was a couple years younger than me sent me an email asking for some advice about his career. He saw me heading into my career full steam ahead and just wanted some simple advice.

What he got was a long email explaining all I had done to set myself up for success and the things I was doing to keep myself and my career headed in the right direction.

I honestly don't remember the entire email. Then we saw each other for the first time in probably 10 years. He was now a successful professional in the field and I had watched his work from far off via social media. One of the first things he mentioned to me was that long email I had sent long ago. He admitted he never expected a reply from me, but he had heeded the advice and it had made a great impact on him.

Of course it was immensely gratifying to know I had helped in some way—however naive and young I might have felt at the time. He had asked. I had answered.

That's how simple it truly is. Be willing and available to give of yourself to someone else simply heading in the same direction as you, albeit a couple of steps behind you.

Get an Intern

One powerful way to take care of yourself and pass on what you've learned is by getting an intern. Bringing someone else on to your team can give you perspective and practical help.

Now let's be clear that it's not just cheap (or free) labor. It's also not just babysitting a college student. A good internship should be a two-way street.

As an employer, you should get quality work from your intern, but you should also expect to spend time investing in their professional development.

As an intern, you can expect to work hard. But you can also expect to learn a lot and get a leg up in your career.

For freelancers, you should consider offering an internship if you think you have something to offer people who are just starting out in your field. That should be the primary consideration: **Can you mentor a newbie?**

Don't get an intern just because you're overworked and need some help. If you need some help, hire someone. **An internship is a trade-off between productive work and professional investment.**

A few more reasons why you might want an internship:

- **Supervisor Experience** - An internship can be a way to develop your own supervisor skills. If you've never managed anyone before, this can be a good way to start.

- **Test Expansion** - If you're considering expanding your freelance operations by hiring someone, an internship can be a good (and temporary) way to test the waters. Employing other people will change the nature of your work. If you're unsure about it, give it a trial run.

- **Recruitment** – If you regularly hire people, interns are a great way to have a ready pool of talent.

- **Good Word of Mouth** – Giving back always generates good will. By hiring interns you're creating opportunities in your field and people will take notice. You're being a good business neighbor.

What Your Intern Can Do

If you think bringing in an intern might be a good move for your company, you should first see what work you have for them to do. How much work do you think you could honestly hand off to a student?

Make a list of all the tasks you could pass off. Focus on the stuff you don't like doing or find tedious. Not so you can load up the intern with menial tasks, but because that's where beginners need to start. If there are easy tasks that are well below your skill level, that's a realistic place for an intern to start. They should be handling some of your grunt work.

But also look for more challenging projects that can stretch an intern's skill. Maybe you don't want to trust an intern with an entire project, but is there a self-contained part of the project you can let them tackle?

How much work you come up with might determine how involved the internship is. Some internships are full time. Others are just part time and can be a good way for a newbie to get their feet wet.

How to Make the Most of an Intern

Once you decide you're up for an intern and you figure out what they can do, you need to make the most of this relationship. You'll need to put some work into it to make sure it's a win for everybody.

- **Clear Goals** – Every project you give your intern should have clear objectives and deadlines. What do you want them to do? When is it due? Do you have specific expectations?

Make sure all of those are clearly communicated. Sometimes you need to over-communicate.

- **Regular Check-Ins** – You're handing your work over to a newbie—you better check in with them often to field questions, course correct and just see how they're doing. You can back off if things are going well, but that's better than checking in too late and find out they're doing it wrong.

- **Be Available** – Those regular check-ins are important, but don't force your intern to save all their questions until your weekly meeting. Be available to answer questions as they come up, either with an open door, instant messaging or whatever works for you. This will help your intern stay on track and deliver work the way you want it.

- **What Do They Need?** – A good way to make the internship experience beneficial for everyone is to figure out what your intern needs and help them get it. What are their career ambitions? Where do they need more experience? Find ways to give them that on-the-job experience. Getting the most out of your intern requires giving them your most (it's a two-way street).

- **Pour Into Them** – Assignments for your intern shouldn't just be work projects that benefit you. Help educate them about the industry. Require them to blog, start using Twitter, set up a LinkedIn profile. Whatever you think is helpful, show them how to do it.

- **Give Praise** – Remember to praise your intern when they're doing good work. Positive reinforcement can do wonders. It will create a better work environment, creates a positive feedback loop and will result in better work all around. Don't let your intern wonder if they're doing a good job or not.

- **Network** – Teach your intern how to network. It's not a skill they usually teach in college, but it's crucial. Meet a colleague for coffee and take your intern along.
  Help them set up an informational interview with someone in the industry. Take them to local meetup groups and introduce them to people.

- **Give Back** – It depends on the industry, but a lot of internships aren't compensated very well or at all. If your compensation isn't great, then make up for it by giving back when you can. Pay for the coffee when you have meetings, buy any books you recommend for the job, take your intern out to lunch once in a while. You are taking away from your time by investing in an intern and they should be grateful, but they're also giving up a higher paid job or a better opportunity. So show that you're grateful too. It's a two-way street.

You might have noticed that a lot of these ways to get the most out of your intern involve more of what you can give to your intern. That's how it works. Yes, you want to get good work out of your intern. But an intern is not a regular employee. They're here to learn. The more you can invest in them and deliver for them, the better work they're going to deliver. If you deliver a rock star internship experience, you'll create a rock star intern.

How an Intern Can Make the Most of an Internship

There are lots of things an intern should know about how to make the most of an opportunity. They can figure that out somewhere else. But there's one thing your intern should know, and you need to make sure they know it:

What an intern gets out of an internship is up to them.

You can provide an incredible internship and do everything in your power to make it an incredible experience.

But your intern is only going to get out of it as much as they put into it.

They have to tell you what they need. They have to own up to their inexperience and be willing and open to grow. If they want to waffle about their career path, then there's not a lot you can do.
If they're not open about where they want to go, you can't do much to help get them there.

If they're not willing to go above and beyond the call of duty to deliver, then you're not going to go above and beyond to deliver for them.

An internship is a two-way street (sensing a theme?).

How to Get an Intern
So how do you actually get an intern? This might be the trickier part. The right situation doesn't always come along.

- **Be Findable** – If a college student did a local search for web designers would they find you? Make sure you're visible.

- **Make It Known** – A low-key way to start looking for an intern is to let people know you're looking. Ask around on social media. Put a job description up on your site and invite people to apply. You don't have to roll out the banners, but simply make it known that you're looking.

- **Advertise** – If you're serious about it, go beyond just making it known and advertise it. List the position on job board sites. Look for intern listings and add your name.

- **Reach Out** – If you want to find a good connection, you'll need to reach out. Contact the appropriate department at local colleges and let them know you're looking for strong, motivated students.

A lot of schools have a career services department, and that might be a good place to start. But be sure to contact the computer science or tech department too. Sometimes students don't always make it out of their departments and down to career services. And sometimes the well-meaning folks in career services know nothing about your industry and won't realize they're sending you the wrong candidates.

Consider an Internship

Bringing on an intern isn't for everyone. Not all of us can be teachers. Some of us don't have the patience or the time or the temperament. But some of us do. For some of us, it will be like something you didn't realize you were missing.

Story: Intern Out of Nowhere
KEVIN D. HENDRICKS, FREELANCE WRITER, MONKEY OUTTA NOWHERE

I've been a one-man freelance shop for a decade now. I've never had any interest in complicating my life by managing employees. So it's been the life of the loner for me. It's worked pretty well since I'm a work-at-home dad.

But all that changed this spring when I received an email from a college student asking about an internship. I had never considered having an intern before and I thought, why not? If they were willing to work with my conditions—unpaid, off-site, provide your own computer—it might be worth trying.

I always thought an intern would be too much work. I didn't want to babysit a college student, and I didn't trust handing my work off to someone else. And that's a potential danger.

But in my situation there were two factors working in favor of an intern:

1. She had the drive to ask me about an internship out of the blue. That showed me she was a self-starter I wouldn't have to babysit.
2. When I called her references, the number one thing I wanted to know was if she was responsible. I didn't care if she knew WordPress, I cared if she handed her work in on time.

The answer: A resounding yes.

So I moved forward knowing I had a responsible candidate. She was motivated and willing to do the work.

I ended up with an intern because the opportunity fell in my lap.

But something funny happened: As I started thinking about the internship and mapping out my plans, I got really excited. The idea of having meetings, sharing my insights, and tackling some new projects really energized me.

It gave me the opportunity to reflect on what helped me out early in my career (and what didn't), and how I could share those lessons with someone else. I really cherished the opportunity.

And it was totally worth it. For 12 weeks this summer I had an intern. It was great. I got to mentor a young student, help her make connections and learn the ropes. I had extra help over the summer, an opportunity to test and sharpen my skills, and a chance to get some needed perspective on projects I'd been putting off.

I got my own start with an unpaid internship 16 years ago at a magazine in Chicago. It gave me the experience and confidence I needed, and having an intern of my own was an opportunity to give back.

This is why you should have an internship. If something like this excites you and rejuvenates your work, do it.

Get to It

We've covered a lot of the ins and outs of freelancing, but at some point you need to get to work. Somewhere along the way all your planning and thinking and dreaming needs to translate into action.

You've got to do the work.

- You need to ship your code. The only way you get paid is by shipping what you do.
- You need the right tools to get the job done. Make sure you've got what you need.
- You're on your own, so you'll need to be your own project manager.
- Finally, ignore the distractions and do the work.

Ship

All good programmers ship. So always ship your code.

Be someone of action and execution, not just a daydreamer or academic who just talks about theory and what could be but never produces. Finish the projects you start and ship them.

Ship because you want to change the world with your code and make people's lives awesome. Code that never ships never has the chance to change the world.

And if you never ship, your code is simply a narcissistic art project, not something intended to change the world. In this sense, code that hasn't shipped doesn't exist because it's not available for the world, just you.

Shipping is bold, brave and for the select few who want to have impact in the real world.

Getting your code into the wild is extremely satisfying. You get to see if people care or not, if you were right or wrong about the decisions and assumptions you've made.

Be known as someone who ships good code and then iterates fast to make it even better.

Understand what a version 1 truly is. We know you can build version 500. But version 1 actually ships and has the chance to be used in the wild. Learn about an MVP (minimum viable product), via The Lean Startup[60]. Also the concepts written about by Jason Fried in *Rework* are invaluable in this context, particularly under the "Progress" heading.

Beware of perfectionism—it's evil and is a farce that can kill your career. Yes, other coders will judge you, but while they are doing that, they aren't shipping. And you are. You're also making your code better while they continue to puff out hot air.

And by the way, they also don't ultimately matter anyway. They aren't your users and customers and your team. (They are just noise actually. And those who have enough time to critique are typically those who never do anything of value in the world but, yeah, critique.)

---

60   http://theleanstartup.com/

Do good solid work, test the hell out of it, then ship the damn thing.

A Quick Word on Deadlines

Deadlines are good and valuable. Don't fear or loathe them. Seek them and the accountability they afford and use them for the success and growth of your career and the projects you're working on. They give you a goal and mark to hit. Light at the end of the tunnel. And we all need something to work toward.

They force you make important decisions that ultimately should help you ship faster and better. They force you to spend time, energy and focus on what actually matters.

They give you a sense of accomplishment. When you and your team members hit deadlines, celebrate. Ring a bell or hit a gong or throw a party for *major* ones, but always recognize them (even to yourself).

Use them! Use them to ship your work. And if you aren't given timelines or milestones, *ask* for them. Or set them for yourself and do the insane thing of sharing them with others. The accountability is good for you and the project.

Toys & Tools

When it's time to get work done, you need the right toys and tools to be productive. Don't short-change yourself. While you shouldn't splurge on toys, you do need the right tools for the right job.

Here are some tips on the tools you need to be a successful freelancer:

- **Good computer:** A good computer is standard equipment for a freelancer these days. It's essential. So don't short-change yourself. It's tempting to be a cheapskate and save a few bucks on a cheap machine or try to make your old system last longer. But don't forget all the time you're wasting with a slow computer.

Or the sanity you're losing every time your computer crashes. Every little hiccup adds up and it has a price. Sometimes it's cheaper to just buy the better computer. "These are the tools you use to do your job," says Basecamp's Jason Fried. "You should have the best you can afford."

- **Smaller screen:** These days computer screens keep getting bigger and bigger. But smaller might be better.
  Jason Fried used to have a 30-inch monitor he'd hook up to his laptop, but now he sticks to the laptop screen. "One screen all the time," he says. "I also like the smaller screen because it forces me to make better use of the space. I found myself getting messy on a 30 inch."

- **More screens:** Or you could go with Stefan Didak's setup[61]: Five monitors, and turn around for at least four more. He claims all that screen real estate makes him more efficient. An old Microsoft study backs him up, showing between a 9% and 50% improvement[62] in productivity.

- **Backup:** You don't have an IT department to bail you out, so you need to backup your own stuff. We're going to recommend you backup your WordPress site, but backing up your computer is important too. Get an external hard drive and start an automatic backup system so you don't have to think about it.

- **Backup plan:** What do you do if your computer dies? Backing up your files is important, but you also need a plan to get back to work. Do you have a secondary computer you can use? Are you saving up for the day you need to replace your computer— especially if that day comes early? Freelance WordPress developer Bill Erickson now keeps spare computers lying around:

---

61   http://www.stefandidak.com/office/

62   http://research.microsoft.com/en-us/news/features/vibe.aspx

"I learned this the hard way when my old Macbook Air became unusably slow (overheating, so the system reduced the processing power by like 80% to try to decrease heat). After a week of barely getting my work done, I bought a mini to use while my computer was in the shop."

- **Get help:** Sometimes stuff breaks on your computer. You don't have time to waste figuring it out, so being able to call tech support whenever you need them might be worth the money. Pony up for Apple Care or whatever extra support plan PCs can access. If it saves your sanity and keeps your computer running, you're saving money. That's totally worth it.

- **Work remotely:** Just because you work from home doesn't mean you have to be at home. You should be able to work remotely. What do you do if the power goes out? What happens when your neighbor is getting a new roof and there's nothing but hammering all day long? Will you still be able to get work done? Not if you're stuck at your desk. Have a laptop handy so you can work on the go. Have files set up so you can access them online if you need to, or at least be able to easily move them to Dropbox or another cloud-based system.

- **Passwords:** These days passwords are important, but there are far too many passwords to ever remember. Use a password service like 1Password or LastPass to store your passwords. You use a lot of online services when you work from home and there's no need to waste brain power on all those passwords.

- **Embrace the cloud:** There are lots of cloud-based services that can make working at home pretty sweet. Experiment with new services, figure out what works and don't be afraid to pay for what you need. Dropbox, Evernote, Skype, Tweetdeck, Google Drive, Trello—whatever works for you.

- **Cloud software:** Even your regular old software is going to the cloud. Microsoft Office and Adobe Creative Suite both have cloud-based, subscription offerings. If you're not using these programs on a regular basis, this might be a cheaper way to get access to what you need.

- **App distraction:** There are always cool new apps to try out that will make you more organized, improve efficiency and make you better looking. But they don't always work out. Try stuff and see what works, but don't jump on every new productivity app. If it ain't broke, don't fix it.

- **Ahoy hoy:** Keeping in touch while you work from home is important, so you need a reliable phone line. A landline may not be necessary, but you may not want to rely on your cell phone. A VOIP option might be a cheaper way to go.

- **Spare phone:** Just like you might need a spare computer, you might also need a spare phone. If the power goes out or your Internet goes down, your VOIP phone line is useless. You'll wish you had a cell phone. And if you can't find your cell or the charger has gone missing, you'll wish you still had that old landline. Consider keeping some sort of secondary phone line just in case.

- **Headsets:** Be sure you have the proper headset for conference calls and hands-free note taking.

- **High speed Internet:** When you work from home you obviously need good Internet service. But think long term. So many cable and telecom companies offer great introductory rates these days, but they don't advertise what the actual price is 6, 12 or 18 months later. Think long term.

- **Printer/Scanner/Fax/Copier:** One of the downsides to working at home is you no longer have access to the industrial copier at work. But the desktop combos work great. Don't settle for just a printer. The scanner/copier function will be incredibly useful when you need to copy invoices, receipts and more. And while you rarely need a fax machine these days, it's nice to have when you need it.

- **Security:** Just because you're at home doesn't mean corporate security doesn't apply. Be professional with sensitive documents: "It's important to adhere to the same confidentiality rules that would apply if you worked at your company's offices," says productivity expert Anne McGurty[63]. "Keep a shredder handy to properly dispose of all sensitive documents, and properly maintain all computer and cloud files."

- **Music:** Browsing Spotify all afternoon may be a waste of time, but listening to music can make you more productive[64]. 88% are more accurate and 81% work faster when listening to music. Plus different music can help more with different tasks. So crank it up.

- **Bag it:** If you're regularly going out of the house to get work done, put together a work bag that has everything you need. Pack the pockets with whatever you might need at your temporary office—paperclips, cough drops, headphones, extra business cards, water bottle, spare pens, highlighters, stamps, sticky notes, paper, tissues, power cords, etc. You want to make it easy to get out of the house when you need to.

---

63   http://www.forbes.com/sites/northwesternmutual/2014/08/05/working-from-home-5-tips-for-being-more-productive-remotely/

64   http://www.prsformusic.com/aboutus/press/latestpressreleases/Pages/new-research-shows-music-hits-the-right-notes-for-business-success.aspx

Story: No

CURTIS MCHALE, FREELANCE DEVELOPER

What are your favorite productivity tools?

The word 'no.' Seriously. I say no a lot.

I only schedule calls on Tuesdays. I'll do one interview per week (like this one) and do all new client calls and existing client meetings on Tuesdays. I don't take meetings the rest of the week. If I have a weekly project I'll do meetings at 9 a.m. or 1 p.m., and then they can't last more than 45 minutes.

It's hard sometimes. But that's how you're going to get work done.

I also say no to email first thing in the morning. I'll check it later in the afternoon. All email is good for in the morning is telling you what other people's priorities are for *your* day.

My phone doesn't beep for email. There are no badges or alerts or anything. The only things that come through are phone calls and text messages. If it's outside work hours and you're not grouped as a friend, I won't answer it. There are times when I really need to focus and I'll turn off the phone. If there's a real emergency my wife will come upstairs and get me or I'll hear the wailing.

I even uninstalled Twitter on a bunch of my devices. It's too easy to be distracted. I'd be reading a book on my iPad and flip over to Twitter, and that's a total waste of time. I deleted all the social networks on my iPad.

Now I still find value in Twitter—I absolutely do. Last year I attributed $20,000 of income to contacts I made on Twitter. But it's about using it appropriately. In the evening with the kids, I put my phone up on the microwave and not in my pocket so I can be present with my kids.

You need to be intentional. I wasted hours a day when I first started. You think, "I'm a freelancer, I can take the dog for a walk." But then it takes two hours to walk the dog. You can waste most of a day doing that.

Project Management

Project management is a freelancer's best friend. You have to be organized and stay on top of your projects. That's a given. But as a WordPress developer, have you considered doing your project management in the site itself? WordPress project management can be a way to merge your love of WordPress with your need to be organized.

You can do all kinds of things with WordPress today, and being WordPress fanatics (you know you are too), we love the idea of WordPress project management.

Benefits of Project Management Systems

If you've been doing freelance WordPress development for any length of time you understand the need for a project management system. You need something to keep you organized and on track, and generally a post-it note won't cut it.

Some of the most-loved benefits of project management systems include:

- **Organization** – Keep track of what needs to be done when. Don't let anything slip through the cracks again.

- **Deadlines** – Moving a project forward means keeping an eye on the due dates. Juggling multiple deadlines can get crazy, and that's where project management really shines.

- **Collaborate** – Few people work in the same office these days and can share a whiteboard together. Collaboration has to happen remotely and you need an online system to make that happen. Some systems restrict that interaction to your team, while others invite outside clients into the process.

- **Archive** – Collaboration is key, but you need to keep track of those conversations. A bunch of email discussions or decisions made in a chat window are great, but it's hard to find those again when you need them. A good project management system archives those conversations and decisions so you can go back and find them in one place.

- **Reporting** – Every client wants to know where a project is at, and a good project management system either lets you know so you can update the client or tells the client directly.

Other Project Management Options

There are loads of project management options out there. Basecamp is the standard. We prefer Trello in the iThemes office. Sometimes it's easier to keep your project management separate or let someone else build it. Sometimes you're busy with clients, and you don't have time to build your own.

But the real benefit to WordPress project management is you can set it up just how you like it. Few other options give you the flexibility of a WordPress project management solution.

Make It Work For You

For project management to be effective in your freelance development, it needs to work for you. If it's frustrating or distracting, it's not saving you any time. You need something that can work the way you want to work.

Sometimes that's easier said than done. How do you want to work? What's the most effective way to do it? What's going to create the least amount of extra work and bureaucracy?

Sometimes you need to think through how something might work, maybe even try a few different ways of doing it, before you settle on the method for you.

Here are some questions you can ask to help figure out what you need:

- **Internal or External?** – Do you want your project management to be primarily internal for your team only, or do you want to include external partners like clients? It can be part of your process to include clients in the project management, but it also means you need to keep things professional. If you want a more casual, laid-back project management system, you might not want to invite your clients in to see the mess.

- **Front End or Back End?** – Do you want something smooth and polished to look good on the front end? Or do you just need something for yourself on the back end?

- **Single or Multiple Projects?** – Do you need to keep your projects separated, or do you want to see details across all your projects? For example, do you want to look at a calendar with dates for only one project at a time, or do you want to see all your project deadlines (or do you want to be able to see both)?

- **What Do You Manage?** – What are you looking to manage? Do you want to-do lists, milestones, a place to schedule deadlines, a place to track conversations, a place to upload files? Figure out which features you need and which ones you don't.

- **Any Extras?** – Are there any extra components you track elsewhere that might make sense to tie into project management? Maybe you track your time or chart budgets, and it'd make sense to see that info there. You don't want to over-complicate things, but if it works for you it might be a good move.

The point is to figure out what works for you. Just because someone set up a project management system to work a certain way doesn't mean you should work that way.

Get Organized & Get Work Done

The whole point of all this project management is to help you get work done. Be careful that you're not getting lost in a rabbit hole of organization and process, creating more bureaucracy than actually getting anything done.

Figure out what you need, find or build the tool that works best, and get work done.

Do the Work

It's easy to be distracted as a freelancer. Those beautiful days in the spring when it finally gets nice out are productivity killers. It's easy to push the work aside and go outside. It's also tempting to make your own schedule—sleep in and work late or take the morning off and work into the evening—and suddenly you're shorting yourself and not getting enough work done.

The beauty of freelancing is that you can make those choices.

You can decide to take a day off to enjoy the weather or go see a new movie in the middle of the day. But you also have to make the sacrifice on the other end and work late or work on a Saturday. You'll never get paid if you don't do the work. So make sure you're doing the work. There's no boss to check in and make sure you're on time— you're the boss. That gives you a lot of freedom, but it also gives you a lot of responsibility.

Story: Do the Work

JARED ATCHISON, FREELANCE DEVELOPER

What advice do you have for budding WordPress freelancers?

Running your own business is awesome. It's very rewarding and with some hard work and planning, your business can be extremely successful.

The key there is hard work. You have to be ready to put in the time, especially at the beginning. The time to: foster knowledge, build a brand, gather leads, network, build relationships, etc. It's hard work and it's not done overnight. If anyone else tells you otherwise, they are full of it.

Also, I think reading tutorials, blogs, and social feeds is important. However, one thing I can't stress enough is that only goes so far. I see way too many people reading instead of doing. At the end of the day, taking action is going to give you the most valuable experience.

Get off social media and start working. Seriously.

Most of the WordPress freelancers out there that are killing it, keep a low profile. They don't keep Twitter open all day or watch Facebook groups. They aren't constantly monitoring the WordPress news sites. Not at all. Instead, they are building things. They are investing that time into improving their business.

I know this because not only do I know many of these freelancers personally, but also I can personally attest to this. When I finally started paying attention to (and addressing) how my time was spent, my revenue and profits both went up considerably.

Now I catch up on Twitter during lunch or in the evenings on my tablet—I don't open the desktop app during the week. The same goes for Facebook and similar services. I read blogs and news sites once or twice a week in the evenings using my RSS feed reader app. I use a service called RescueTime that helps me keep tabs on how my time is spent and make sure I don't fall back into bad habits.

I believe it is important to network and build relationships. I have a close-knit group of friends who are very successful and/or run their own business. Having these friends has really been invaluable to me both personally and professionally. Personally, I'm a huge believer in surrounding myself with people who are smarter or more successful than I. It pushes me to do more and keeps me from getting complacent.

So whether it's going to local meet-ups, attending WordCamps, finding a mentor, joining a mastermind group—put yourself in a position to build lasting relationships.

Lastly, we all know the benefits of setting goals. However, that's only part of the equation. When you set your goals, don't forget to develop and implement systems that help you achieve them.

Change the World

Going into business as a freelancer makes you part of a special breed. We're naturally ambitious, driven people who take giant leaps many others don't or won't.

We're often labeled "risk takers," "mavericks" and "renegades."

We take bold steps. We understand the potential consequences, but we still blaze trails.

But in the thrill and chase of building our enterprises, sometimes we trample on people and relationships. On purpose or by accident.

The justification goes like this, stripped out of a movie about mobsters: "It's not personal. It's just business." You know, business is business and it's about competition and cutting them off at the knees. Winning at whatever the cost. It's survival of the fittest, where the only best, strongest, or fastest, or rather the cutthroat, ruthless and heartless should exist in the end.

But that's B.S.

Business is always personal.

"It's just business," is actually counterintuitive and detrimental to succeeding in business. In other words let's say it more bluntly: it's stupid and outdated.

If you burn bridges and take all you can get, you're going to be all alone. No one will want to do business with you. Your clients will go elsewhere and your partners will turn away.

As an entrepreneur, you have a higher calling.

Entrepreneurs can and should change the world. And we should most certainly leave it better than we found it. There are way too many recent examples of the opposite out there today.

Our work as entrepreneurs is fundamentally about serving and helping other people. You might be going into this for yourself, for your own gain—and that's fine. But if you want to stay in it you need to realize that a freelancer is part of a much larger web. You can screw people over and cut ties until you're all alone, or you can work so that everybody wins.

How to Change the World as a Freelancer

We've already talked about how to write your business plan, how to organize your finances, how to market yourself, how to be professional and how to take care of yourself. We've encouraged you to dive in and get to work. And now it's time to encourage you to do that work in a way that changes the world.

Don't just be any freelancer. Be a world-changing freelancer. Be a freelancer that makes such a difference in people's lives that they clamor to work with you. Here's how to do it…

Do Right

The first and foundational way to change the world as a freelancer is simple:

Do right. By everyone. All the time.

Then, when you screw up (and it will happen), admit it, ask for forgiveness, make amends, learn and grow from it and move on. Way too often we put what's right, last. We know what's right. But too often we choose to ignore what we know is right.

It's as simple as the golden rule: **Do unto others as you'd have them do unto you.**

We ignore the cost, or rather, the damage of doing wrong to people. Yet at the same time we'd be outraged if we were treated in the same manner by others.

Like doctors, freelancers should go by the credo, **"Do no harm".**

This new rule applies to your clients, contractors, partners, community, industry—anyone involved in or affected by your business.

Questions That Can Help

If you need help making consistently good decisions that do right by people, here is a list of questions you can run through:

- Why do I really want to make this decision? What are my motivations? What spurred me to make this decision?
- Who will this decision benefit most? The least?
- What obligations and responsibilities as a leader, entrepreneur and fellow human being do I have with the people affected by this decision?

- Do I have all the facts and perspectives to make a good, solid decision?
- Have I asked for feedback and input of people I trust and respect who will be honest with me about the decision I'm making?
- Will it permanently damage my relationships with people? Will it harm others as a result? Purposefully? And how wide will the damage be?
- Is it the best, well-informed decision I can make that benefits the most people at the least cost?
- Does this decision put profits over people?
- Is it for short-term gain at the expense of the long term?
- If the circumstances were reversed and I was the one being affected how would I feel about this decision?
- With all this in mind, is this the right decision to make? That'll help you answer if it's right or not.

Do Good

Doing good is always the right thing to do. But doing good is specifically about impact. Positive impact. Making a difference. Changing the world for the better.

It's about making good decisions that count the cost in terms of people. Thinking about and then doing good for others.

It's also about legacy. The good you do today for tomorrow.

Doing good starts with questions like:

- How can I do good in people's lives? Specifically, my customers, my team and my partners?
- How can I do good in my community?
- How can I do good in my industry?

Here are some ways to do good:

Participate

Get active in your community and industry. Engage and support activities that promote a better community. "Part of giving, participating, and mentoring is recognizing that you have something to contribute," says nonprofit marketer Bet Hannon.

Lead

When others complain, step up and lead to make a difference. Give credit where credit is rightly due.

Mentor

Pour yourself into others. Pass on your experience, expertise and time by investing in other people.

Champion

Stand up for what's right and for your customers and team.

Give

Give generously of your time, talent and treasure. Give back when the time comes. And always be paying it forward. Everybody started somewhere, and that includes you.

Care

We could have summed up freelance success in one word:

Care.

If we approach entrepreneurship as a high calling, where we get to share our unique passions and strengths and skills for the betterment of others, then we should naturally care.

Caring is about empathy—being able to "understand and share the feelings of another."

Caring is about showing kindness, compassion and concern for other people involved in or affected by your business.

Caring is other-centered. It means being genuinely interested in *their* stories, not your own.

And yes, it gets messy when you care. You become invested and can get hurt. Other people open up their lives to you. Nobody said it was easy.

Here are some simple ways you can show you care:

- **Ask about them and their unique stories first.** Don't dominate the conversations about you, your work and what they should buy from you. And as they are opening up to you, don't be scanning the room for other people to talk to!

- **Treat *all* people like human beings with immense value.** No one is insignificant. Everybody matters. You'd be surprised how awful receptionists or assistants are treated, but guess who actually has the ear of the influencers?

- **Remember names and stories.** It's great when someone remembers your name. Make an effort to remember names. We all blank out from time to time, so try to remember a name beforehand. When in doubt, admit it and reintroduce yourself.

- **Follow-up when you hear about good or bad news.** Don't be the person who only ever cares about business. Ask about someone's accomplishments or how you can help when they're having a hard time.

- **Be transparent and open about your own personal stories, vulnerabilities and flaws (when appropriate).** You'll be surprised how often people reciprocate when you open up. It shows you're human and it builds connections.

By the way, caring breeds loyalty.

Caring also brings you more in alignment with what your clients want. When you care about them, you empathize with and for them, uniquely understanding who they are and what they want and need. Your stories will be more aligned, and your products and services will cater more to them because, yes, you care.

Be Genuine & Authentic

Oscar Wilde said, "Be you, everybody else is taken."

You are the original. So be the original. The honest and real version of who you really are.

Be the WYSIWYG version of you. "What-you-see-is-what-you-get."

In a world filled with bogus caricatures, simply being you will earn more respect and trust than you can imagine.

The "real deal" honesty is refreshing for people.

One of the most challenging things for entrepreneurs, especially successful ones, is keeping our egos in check.

It's easy to get hooked into becoming someone we're not.

So let's be honest, you're not Steve Jobs and your company certainly isn't Apple. You're not Richard Branson or Virgin either.

And Entourage was just a show on HBO.

So let's stop pretending we're something we're not and instead be the real deal—the one-of-a-kind you.

Here are some thoughts about being the original:

- Being real and being you is simply easier. It takes less energy, focus, time and resources you could use for long-term gains for you and others.
- Illusions aren't sustainable. When they eventually fade or flicker, you're just found to be a fraud.

- We all crave genuine relationships and intimacy. When you're playing a part and wearing a mask, you can't have either.

- You'll win fans, followers and friends. It's increasingly refreshing to find people who are authentic and real because it gives us permission to also be ourselves. Thus, people will actually want to spend time with you because you're not trying to fool them.

Be Open & Honest

It's ingrained in us to keep secrets and to share little or no information about what we do or why we do it.

But upfront, open and honest communication about the why and what is truly the best policy for most decisions and situations.

There will be temptations as a freelancer to be less than honest. You'll make a mistake and want to cover it up. Or you'll face a decision to cheat or lie. It'll start small. But if you justify it to yourself, another temptation will come along and the dishonesty will snowball.

Before you know it you've stepped into territory you never thought
you would enter.

Honesty is the best policy.

Whenever you make mistakes—and we all do—own up to them.
Correct them as best you can and move on.

Don't lie or cheat or steal. You have to trust clients and they have to
trust you, so be trustworthy.

Here are some lessons about being open and honest in business:

- **Most people simply want to know the what and the why.** As
  best you can, share those details. "Here is what happened…" and,
  "Here's why we decided this…". They won't always be happy about
  your decision or agree with it, but at least they know you're being
  open, honest and forthright about it.

- **It shows you have nothing to hide.** When you don't
  communicate at all, it promotes cynicism and doubt. In a vacuum
  of details, people will conjure up the worst.

- **Use it to showcase your principles and values.** It demonstrates
  your moral compass.

- **Do it to keep earning the trust and respect of those we serve.**
  Just being open and honest and sharing the why behind your
  decisions earns loyalty and trust—keys to leading people and
  growing a business.

Serve Others

You've achieved that elusive freelancer freedom and you no longer
answer to anybody else, right? You are your own boss and don't have
to serve anybody else, right?

Not so fast. Yes, you've got your glorious freedom, but it's going to be glorious poverty if you act like a jerk and nobody wants to work with you.

Working with others, whether it's clients, contractors or anybody else, is a two-way street. We all serve each other.

If you want to be treated right, you need to treat others right. Your clients serve you by paying their bills, providing content, giving feedback and hopefully doing it all on time. You serve your clients by delivering a quality product, also hopefully on time. It's a back and forth process.

Never forget that even though you are your own boss, you still need to serve others.

It's not totally unselfish, nor is it totally selfish. It's just being a good human being that also cares about others.

Here are some additional tips for serving others:

- **Approach your business with an attitude of mutual service.** It is infectious.

- **Show others preference and priority.** Let others go first in the lunch line. Open doors for them. Give them your undivided attention.

- **Be willing to do what you ask others to do.** Take out the trash. Respond in a timely manner. Meet deadlines.

- **Respect and value people in their service to others.** Everybody can and should contribute. And even if their contribution might not be as big or valuable as another's, show that you value them for their service and contribution.

- **Weed out the selfish.** Serving others doesn't mean you're a door mat. It's a two-way street and if someone isn't willing to serve, move on.

Selfish Benefits of Playing by the Rules

Caring, serving, doing good and right—all of these things take time and energy. And a lot of it.

Sometimes they even will cost you money or momentum, especially in the short term. They will become a burden to you and quickly discarded if you don't see them for what they are: **investments in people.** The best investments you can make are in people. They don't all pay off. Some investments flop fabulously or blow up in your face. People can and will disappoint you. (And you'll disappoint others.) But for those investments that do pay off, they pay richly.

You'll become a magnet for quality people. **Do good and right by people consistently, and you will attract quality team members, partners and, yes, even clients.**

Clients want to know you believe in something, that you stand for something and that at the basic level, you'll do what you say you'll do for them too.

Good, quality people are drawn to other good, quality people because we're playing with the same rulebook that says we respect and value each other. We want the best for each other.

So do right.

Do good.

Care.

Be genuine and authentic, open and honest.

Serve others.

Invest in people and they will invest in you, your business, your vision.

And in this case, everybody's going to win. Big.

Closer: Get to Work

So you want to be a freelancer? Now you know the ins and outs. It's a challenging job, full of ups and downs. But you can do it. Just be prepared. Don't be discouraged. Always keep learning.

We've just given you loads to think about, and now you have some goals to make. Set some goals for yourself and get to work. People who make goals are the people who meet their goals. People who prepare for the worst can survive anything. Stick with it and don't freak out when things get tough. You planned for it, remember?

And know that it gets easier. Once you have success you'll build momentum and more jobs will come in. It does get easier.

Now get to work.

Tools to Help You Start and Grow Your Freelance Web Design Business

Since 2008, we've been creating WordPress plugins, themes and training for freelancers, marketers, entrepreneurs, web designers and developers. We want to help take the guesswork out of building, maintaining, securing and running WordPress websites.

BackupBuddy
The original WordPress backup plugin that backs up, restores and moves your WordPress sites

Sync
Manage all your WordPress sites from one convenient dashboard.

iThemes Security

Our WordPress security plugin to secure and protect your WordPress sites.

Exchange

Sell your stuff online in 5 minutes or less with our WordPress ecommerce plugin.

Builder

Build WordPress sites quickly and easily with our DIY WordPress theme framework.

iThemes Training

Professional web design training with WordPress.

We want you to prosper as a result of our work, products, training and resources.

Check out iThemes.com for more information.

Resources

For an interactive list of links and resources included in this book, visit: https://ithemes.com/ultimate-guide-starting-freelance-web-design-business

Books

The $100 Startup: Reinvent the Way You Make a Living, Do What You Love, and Create a New Future by Chris Guillebeau

Anything You Want: 40 Lessons for a New Kind of Entrepreneur by Derek Sivers

Book Yourself Solid: The Fastest, Easiest, and Most Reliable System for Getting More Clients Than You Can Handle by Michael Port

Content Rules: How to Create Killer Blogs, Podcasts, Videos, Ebooks, Webinars (and More) That Engage Customers and Ignite Your Business by Ann Handley & C.C. Chapman

Dave Ramsey's Complete Guide to Money: The Handbook of Financial Peace University by Dave Ramsey

Do the Work: Overcome Resistance and Get Out of Your Own Way by Steven Pressfield

Duct Tape Marketing: The World's Most Practical Small Business Marketing Guide by John Jantsch

The E-Myth: Why Most Small Businesses Don't Work and What to Do About It by Michael Gerber

EntreLeadership: 20 Years of Practical Business Wisdom From the Trenches by Dave Ramsey

Get Clients Now: A 28-Day Marketing Program for Professionals, Consultants, and Coaches by C.J. Hayden

Guerrilla Marketing: Easy and Inexpensive Strategies for Making Big Profits From Your Small Business by Jay Conrad Levinson and Jeannie Levinson

Launch: How to Quickly Propel Your Business Beyond the Competition by Michael A. Stelzner

The Leadership Challenge: How to Make Extraordinary Things Happen in Your Organization by James Kouzes and Barry Posner

The Lean Startup: How today's Entrepreneurs Use Continuous Innovation to Create Radically Successful Businesses by Eric Ries

Little Bets: How Breakthrough Ideas Emerge From Small Discoveries by Peter Sims

Never Get a "Real" Job: How to Dump Your Boss, Build a Business and Not Go Broke by Scott Gerber

On Writing Well: The Classic Guide to Writing Nonfiction by William Zissner

The Price is Right: An Introduction to Product Pricing by Chris Lema

The Power of Cult Branding: How 9 Magnetic Brands Turned Customers Into Loyal Followers (and Yours Can, Too!) by Matthew W. Ragas and Bolivar J. Bueno

The Referral Engine: Teaching Your Business to Market Itself by John Jantsch

Remote: Office Not Required by Jason Fried and David Heinemeier Hansson

Rework by Jason Fried and David Heinemeier Hansson

Standout: The Groundbreaking New Strengths Assessment From the Leader of the Strengths Revolution by Marcus Buckingham

Start With Why: How Great Leaders Inspire Everyone to Take Action by Simon Sinek

StrengthsFinder 2.0 by Tom Rath

Success for Dummies by Zig Ziglar

Switch: How to Change Things When Change Is Hard by Chip Heath and Dan Heath

The Ultimate Sales Machine: Turbocharge Your Business With Relentless Focus on 12 Key Strategies by Chet Holmes

Why Johnny Can't Brand: Rediscovering the Lost Art of the Big Idea by Bill Schley and Car Nichols Jr.

Free iThemes Ebooks

A growing collection of free ebooks are available from iThemes. Here are some of the most applicable for freelancers:

11 Things to Do With Every New WordPress Install - https://ithemes.com/publishing/11-things-every-new-wordpress-install/

15 Best Practices for Rockin' Webinars - http://ithemes.com/publishing/15-best-practices-for-rockin-webinars/

Blogging Isn't Dead: Discovering (or Rediscovering) the Power of Blogging - http://ithemes.com/publishing/blogging-isnt-dead-ebook/

Ecommerce for Everybody: You've Got Something to Sell - https://ithemes.com/publishing/ecommerce-everybody/

The Ecommerce Opportunity: How Freelance Developers Can Build Ecommerce Websites With WordPress - https://ithemes.com/publishing/wordpress-ecommerce-opportunity/

Getting Started With Google Analytics - http://ithemes.com/publishing/getting-started-with-google-analytics/

Getting Started With BackupBuddy - https://ithemes.com/publishing/getting-started-with-backupbuddy/

Go Mobile With WordPress: Exploring the New Mobile Reality for Website Owners - https://ithemes.com/publishing/go-mobile-with-wordpress/

Hiring Your First Employee: A Step-by-Step Guide - https://ithemes.com/publishing/hiring-your-first-employee-step-step-guide/

How to Create Your First Ebook: From Initial Idea to Ready for Readers - https://ithemes.com/publishing/how-to-create-your-first-ebook/

How to Run a WordPress Meetup: Tips for Running a Successful Local WordPress Meetup - http://ithemes.com/publishing/run-wordpress-meetup/

Join the Club: How to Create a Membership Site - https://ithemes.com/publishing/join-the-club-how-to-create-a-membership-site/

Turning Contacts Into Contracts - https://ithemes.com/publishing/turning-contacts-into-contracts/

See the whole list: https://ithemes.com/publishing/

Freelancer Interviews
We've interviewed a number of freelance WordPress developers and included pieces of their stories in this book. You can find the full interviews on the iThemes blog:

Jared Atchison - Part 1: https://ithemes.com/2014/06/23/freelance-wordpress-developer-jared-atchison-getting-started/, Part 2: https://ithemes.com/2014/06/30/freelance-wordpress-developer-jared-atchison-best-practices/

Brian Casel - https://ithemes.com/2014/08/06/web-designer-brian-casel-offers-advice-freelancers/

Dave Clements - https://ithemes.com/2014/05/27/selling-wordpress-maintenance-dave-clements/

Carrie Dils - https://ithemes.com/2014/09/12/freelance-wordpress-developer-carrie-dils/

Bill Erickson - https://ithemes.com/2014/04/14/freelance-wordpress-developer-bill-erickson-1/

Dan King - https://ithemes.com/2014/05/20/selling-wordpress-maintenance-dan-king/

Curtis McHale - https://ithemes.com/2014/06/13/freelance-wordpress-developer-curtis-mchale/

Andrew Norcross - https://ithemes.com/2015/01/26/andrew-norcross-wordpress-developer/

Justin Sainton - https://ithemes.com/2014/09/05/freelance-wordpress-developer-justin-sainton/

38139303R00182

Made in the USA
San Bernardino, CA
31 August 2016